Working Parents

Life Course Studies
David L. Featherman
David I. Kertzer
   Series Editors

Nancy W. Denney
Thomas J. Espenshade
Dennis P. Hogan
Jennie Keith
Maris A. Vinovskis
   Associate Series Editors

Family and the Female Life Course: The Women of Verviers, Belgium, 1849–1880
George Alter

The Ageless Self: Sources of Meaning in Late Life
Sharon R. Kaufman

Family, Class, and Ideology in Early Industrial France: Social Policy and the Working-Class Family, 1825–1848
Katherine A. Lynch

Working Parents: Transformations in Gender Roles and Public Policies in Sweden
Phyllis Moen

In the U.K.:
Adamantine Studies on the Individual in Society, Number 2.

Working Parents

Transformations in Gender Roles and Public Policies in Sweden

Phyllis Moen

The University of Wisconsin Press
Madison, Wisconsin

Adamantine Press Limited
London, England

The University of Wisconsin Press
114 North Murray Street
Madison, Wisconsin 53715

Published in the United Kingdom by
Adamantine Press Limited
3 Henrietta Street, Covent Garden
London   WC2E 8LU

5   4   3   2   1

Printed in the United States of America

Library of Congress Cataloging-in-Publication Data
Moen, Phyllis.
    Working parents: transformations in gender roles and public
policies in Sweden/Phyllis Moen.
    198 pp.   cm.—(Life course studies)
    Bibliography: p.
    Includes index.
    1. Work and family—Government policy—Sweden. I. Title.
II. Series.
HD4904.25.M64   1989
362.8'28—dc 19   88-40439
ISBN 0-299-12100-3 cloth; ISBN 0-299-12104-6 (pbk.)

British Library Cataloguing in Publication Data

Moen, Phyllis, 1942–
    Working parents: transformations in gender roles and public
    policies in Sweden.—
    (Adamantine studies on the individual in society; no. 2)
    1. Sweden. Working parents I. Title
    306'.36
ISBN 0-7449-0012-3
ISBN 0-7449-0013-1 Pbk

For Dick

Contents

Contents

ix

Figures

Tables

Acknowledgments

A great many people in both Sweden and the United States made it possible for me to write this book, but a few were essential in getting the study launched. Bengt Abrahamsson at the Swedish Center for Working Life (Arbetslivscentrum) in Stockholm invited me to be a visiting professor in 1983, and Henry Persson, then director of Arbetslivscentrum, provided the necessary financial aid, along with the services of an invaluable research assistant, Sisko Bergandorff. Phil Schoggen and Henry Riccuiti of the Department of Human Development and Family Studies, as well as Dean Jerome Zigler and Associate Dean Nancy Saltford of the College of Human Ecology, facilitated my leave of absence from Cornell University.

Sten Johansson, originator of the Level of Living Survey, graciously permitted me to use this remarkable data archive. Robert Erikson, director of the Swedish Institute for Social Research (Institutet för Social Forskning) at Stockholm University, provided ready access to their computing facilities, first in 1983 and again in 1985. Olle Lundberg gave generously of his time and expertise instructing me on the structure of the data set and discussing both theoretical and methodological issues.

Any number of others supplied assistance along the way. Kerstin Wiklund of the Swedish Ministry of Labour, Jan Tröst of Uppsala University, Karin Sandqvist of the Stockholm Institute of Education, and Eva Bernhardt of Stockholm University furnished me with demographic and labor force statistics. Diane Mitchell facilitated translations. Siv Gustafsson, Marianne Sundström, Elizabet Näsman, Ann-Britt Hellmark, Annika Baude, and Wuokko Knocke were stimulating colleagues at Arbetslivscentrum. Still others—Birgit Persson, Birger and Ann-Charlotte Viklund, Bo Hedberg and Birgitta Johansson, Anders and Gunilla Broström, Bertil Gardell, Rut and Olle Hammarström, Greta Hammarström, William and Marianne Peterson, Elizabet Lagerlöff, Gerdt Sundström, Ann Lindgren, Sune and Kristina Ahlén, Patsy Buchman—along with the many people I interviewed, helped me to learn about Sweden and Swedes first-hand.

The Life Cycle Institute at Catholic University in Washington, D.C., provided me with an office during my 1985 sabbatical year. John McCarthy, David Baker, Doug Sloane, and Jim Youniss offered encouragement as well as methodological advice.

My appreciation also to those who read earlier drafts and made valuable suggestions, including Series Editors David Featherman and David Kertzer, as well as Dennis Hogan, Robert Erikson, Sara McLanahan, and Annemette Sorensen. Jan Blakeslee was a wonderful editor, combining insight with a sense of humor. And Irene Pytcher was a model of patience as she constructed and reconstructed the tables and figures.

My intellectual debt is owed to Reuben Hill, who taught me to think as a "comparativist"; Jeylan Mortimer, who shares my interest in the work-family interface; Glen H. Elder, Jr., whose life course perspective has left an indelible imprint on my thinking; and Urie Bronfenbrenner, who exemplifies the possibilities that lie at the intersections of policy and science. Finally, and most important, is my husband Richard P. Shore, who served as my best editor, critic, champion, and friend.

Working Parents

1

Introduction

A fundamental idea embraced today in Sweden is that one must
aim for change which emancipates men as well as women from
the restrictive effects engendered by the traditional sex-roles—
culturally conditioned expectations of an individual on account
of sex. (Palme, 1970)

Revolution in the Family

Employment is now a fact of life for most parents in advanced industrialized societies—mothers as well as fathers. Throughout history this
has been true for fathers, whose principal role in the family has been that
of the "good provider," especially since the Industrial Revolution (Bernard, 1981; Grønseth, 1972). But the increasing labor force participation
of mothers represents a marked departure from their culturally pre-
scribed role as caretaker of children in particular and of the family and
household in general. Women have, of course, always been workers,
wives, and mothers.[1] Now, the timing, duration, and sequencing of these
roles are changing. In particular, the employment of mothers of young
children has come to present one of the major cultural dilemmas of contemporary parenthood: how to meet the challenges posed to individuals
who are simultaneously producers of goods and services and producers
and caretakers of children (e.g., Myrdal and Klein, 1956; Dahlström and
Liljeström, 1969; Kanter, 1977; Pleck, 1977; Smith, 1979; Gerson, 1985).

Being a parent in today's world increasingly entails finding ways of

1. Throughout this book I use the words "working" and "employed" interchangeably, as
is common usage. But I am nonetheless cognizant of the fact that homemakers indeed
"work," though they are not paid for their labor. Here, however, I am concentrating on *paid*
labor force participation.

meshing parenthood and employment for both mothers and fathers. And the changing definitions of gender roles and shifts in the demographics of both the workplace and the family have created an aura of ambiguity about what it means to be a parent and what it means to be a worker.

What *are* the proper roles of mothers and fathers in contemporary society? Are we moving toward a convergence of men's and women's roles both at home and at work? Parenthood has come to occupy only a relatively short period of time in adulthood as a result of reduced fertility and increased longevity (Ariès, 1962; Laslett and Wall, 1972; Uhlenberg, 1980; Cherlin, 1981; Davis, 1984). Employment, in contrast, has become increasingly prominent in the lives of women during their early adult years, as it always has been for men (Smith, 1979; Mason et al., 1976; Thornton and Freedman, 1979; Thornton et al., 1983). Parenthood is inevitably being shaped by the structure and conditions of work, and the resources available for parenting are more than ever a function of those supplied (e.g., income, status) and those required (e.g., time, energy) by the work role.

Clearly, we are living in the midst of a major social revolution, one that is changing not only men's and women's roles but our very concepts of what it means to be a family, a parent, a worker. How, in these last years of the 20th century, can we best fashion new social arrangements by which men and women equitably share family and employment roles and which, at the same time, will meet the needs of children? The Industrial Revolution introduced a sexual division of labor within the family, with middle-class women engaged in domestic activities at home and men working outside the home in order to support the family financially. This development in turn gave birth to a doctrine of "separate spheres," wherein the bifurcation of men's and women's lives became even more pronounced (Degler, 1980; Cott and Pleck, 1979). Liljeström and colleagues (1978) point out:

When industrialization separated homes from workplaces the men's contacts with children were diminished. Childhood ended up in 'women's territory'. The child formed more and more the core of 'meaning' in the married woman's life. . . . No wonder, then, that the mother came to be chained to a pedestal of indispensability. Each parent developed a specialty: the one became a Mother, the other a Breadwinner [p. 105].

But as today's women are increasingly employed outside the home at every life stage, raising children, even when various forms of substitute childcare are available, is becoming more and more problematic. In contemporary society most mothers face a double burden, with responsibilities at work added on to their responsibilities at home. To be sure, fathers have increased their domestic involvement, but not in any major way (Miller and Garrison, 1982; Pleck, 1985; Coverman and Sheley, 1986; Juster, 1985; Robinson, 1985; Nock and Kingston, 1988). Thus, caring for children in a world where both parents are employed is a dilemma confronted thus far principally by women.

The recent, widespread entrance of wives and mothers into the labor force is rapidly emerging as a matter of intense public concern throughout the advanced industrialized world. For society, the employment of mothers has meant, first, a shift in the traditional division of labor that has long been regarded as functional both for the family and for society (Parsons and Bales, 1966; Parsons, 1959), and second, the demand for an accommodation—often slow and reluctant, as in the United States—of public and private sector policies to the new demography of the workplace and the family, wherein workers are parents and parents are workers (Kamerman et al., 1983; Kamerman and Kahn, 1981, 1987; Wilensky, 1981).

Yet jobs in all advanced industrialized countries are structured for individuals, not for family members. Thus, parents are hampered by employment policies and practices, as well as by cultural norms, that engender competition between work and family roles. These conflicts, again, are especially pronounced for women, since men are expected and expect to devote themselves primarily to breadwinning, and that means to their jobs. But the momentum toward gender equality suggests that men's and women's roles both at work and at home are converging. Although the workplace and the home typically are both physically and temporally separate, work and family roles have become inextricably intertwined, as women in the childbearing and child-rearing stages of life sustain their attachment to the labor force. In the face of these transformations the ability of parents to meet the requirements of their employment at the same time that they fulfill the needs of their children becomes increasingly problematic. These potentially conflicting cross-pressures and their implications for both personal well-being and public policy constitute the subject of this book.

Sweden—A Social Model?

The central question remains: can adults manage productive
roles in the labor force at the same time as they fulfill productive
roles within the family—at home? (Kamerman and Kahn, 1981,
p. 2)

Perhaps the best place to seek new models for combining working and parenting is Sweden, the prototypical postindustrial society. Nowhere else to date has a society more effectively addressed the meshing of child-rearing and employment. What makes the Swedish case especially provocative is the concerted effort made by government, organized labor, and other institutions to distribute the burden of parenting between men and women, and to facilitate the employment of all adults, including those caring for infants and children.

Because all advanced societies must eventually confront realities created by the labor force participation of mothers and because there may well be lessons to be learned from the Swedish experience, this book examines the consequences of the changing patterns of work–family relations for Swedish parents of young children. Specifically, the research draws upon data from three consecutive interviews (1968, 1974, 1981) of a representative national sample of Swedish adults, the Level of Living Survey (Erikson and Åberg 1987; Johansson, 1972) to (1) describe the changing nature of the work attachments and employment conditions of parents of preschool children, (2) trace the implications of these changing conditions for personal well-being, and (3) offer evidence about the impact of public policies adopted to make it easier for both men and women to reconcile work and family roles.

The period from 1968 to 1981 saw two important developments in Swedish society. First, there was a major influx of mothers with young children into the labor force. Second, Sweden adopted a number of legislative reforms intended to reconcile the often competing employment and family responsibilities of working parents (Scott, 1982; Wistrand, 1981; Ruggie, 1984; Sundström, 1987).

In examining the Swedish case I have been guided by a "resource approach" to families, one that assumes that parents can successfully fulfill their child-rearing responsibilities only to the degree permitted by their personal resources and structural options (Aldous and Hill, 1969; Gove et al., 1973; Moen, 1982; Moen et al., 1983). The most basic of these resources is, of course, income or, more specifically, purchasing power (cf. Coleman and Rainwater, 1978; Rainwater, 1974a,b). Although the distribution of income among families in Sweden has been and continues to be amply documented (Åberg et al., 1987; Korpi, 1974; Erikson et al., 1987; NCBS, 1982; Johansson, 1972; Fritzell, 1985), there are still other important resources required by parents raising young children—time, energy, health, and psychological well-being—that have commanded much less attention. And vitally affecting the supply of these resources are the working hours and other workplace conditions experienced by employed parents (Piotrowski, 1979; Kohn, 1977; Mott, 1965; Miller et al., 1979; Mortimer, 1976). Concern about family welfare requires that we examine the separate and combined influence of those basic work-

place conditions on the noneconomic resources available to pa
managing their own lives and guiding the lives of their children.[2]

A common thread running through contemporary discussions ... the
United States of changing gender roles is the increasing role overloads and
consequent strains experienced by parents, especially women, who
simultaneously take on work and family obligations (Pleck, 1977, 1985;
Moore and Hofferth, 1979; Bronfenbrenner and Crouter, 1982). Not yet
clear in this discourse are the specific aspects of employment that contribute most to these role strains, whether certain workplace conditions are
particularly troublesome for parents of young children, and the conditions under which parents are most and least able to cope.

The Swedish experience presents an important lesson about the work–
family connection that arguably will be a fact of life in the United States
by the year 2000. At that time the proportion of American mothers of
young children in the labor force will approach that already experienced
in Sweden by the early 1980s. But although the Swedish model may suggest some options to consider in the United States, it cannot offer "whole-
cloth" solutions to the problems we face in this country. Our choices will
depend ultimately on the values that we espouse as well as the particular
constraints imposed by the role of our government and the structure of
our employment system.

A Life Course Perspective

This book locates the phenomenon of parental well-being within a broad
sociological context of social stratification and social change. Fundamental to the study is its life course perspective.[3] This approach emphasizes
the dynamic interconnection of work and family careers. It focuses on
change, in this case the changing roles of men and women and the Swedish family policies aimed at facilitating a convergence of their roles. A key
component of this analytic framework is the concept of *trajectory* or
career. The predicament of working parents grows out of the simultaneous demands of two trajectories: the work career and the family
"career." These interlocking trajectories will become even more intertwined as we move into the twenty-first century and the role of full-time
homemaker approaches obsolescence.

2. I am using the term "welfare" as broadly defined—see Johansson, 1972, 1973; Erikson
and Åberg, 1987; Erikson et al., 1987.

3. The life course perspective is most closely identified with the research and writings of
Glen H. Elder, Jr., but the "life-span" approach shares many of the same concepts. See
Elder, 1974, 1978, 1985; Featherman, 1983.

A second basic concept is that of *transition*, in this case the transition to parenthood, certainly a major turning point in the life course of individuals. The timing and context of this transition obviously determine how it affects well-being. And there is no doubt that in postindustrial society the transition to parenthood is far different from that experienced in the 1950s and 1960s, when childbearing typically led to labor force withdrawal for wives who could afford to do so.

Life course analysis also emphasizes the *context* of lives. Clearly, the impact of the social revolution in gender roles will differ for individuals in accordance with the resources with which they confront these transformations. For example, the relations between the worlds of work and family life obviously take different shapes for women than for men, since women have invaded what once was the male domain of paid employment to a far greater extent than have men taken on traditionally female domestic responsibilities. Moreover, as we shall see, the actual employment conditions of men and women differ appreciably with regard to working hours and schedules, job demands, and workplace flexibility. Thus, fathers and mothers may well occupy similar roles in that they both are in the labor force, but they tend to hold different types of jobs and work under different conditions. Furthermore, even the same workplace conditions may have markedly different effects on men and women, as a function of their gender-role socialization and the differing societal expectations of mothers and fathers.

Still another feature of the life course framework is the need to link individual lives with historical time (e.g., Elder, 1975; Hareven, 1978; Modell et al., 1976), that is, to tie large-scale social changes to changes in the lives of individuals. Social transformations of gender roles have repercussions on the opportunities and constraints experienced by individuals within that society. Conversely, particular individual choices may lead to significant transformations in society as a whole. Therefore, it is important to relate changing definitions of gender roles and Swedish family policies promoting gender equality to the specific experiences of individuals at particular moments in history.

The analysis concentrates on two major sources of strain for parents of young children: working time (particularly hours of employment and, for women, employment history) and working conditions. Parental strain or well-being is gauged by various indicators of psychological health included in the Level of Living survey (reported symptoms of depression, sleeplessness, anxiety, fatigue). It is unquestionably difficult to conceptualize, much less measure, well-being or quality of life in a truly positive sense. Far easier, and the tack taken here, is to focus on the *absence* of well-being, as gauged by indicators of psychological distress and/or physical fatigue.

Throughout the book, several themes recur; they reinforce the life course emphasis on dynamism and context.

Differences over Time. What has remained constant and what has changed from the late 1960s until the early 1980s in the lives and well-being of Swedish parents? This question is particularly important for Americans because in many ways working parents in the United States in the late 1980s resemble those in Sweden in the late 1960s, and by the 1990s trends in the employment of mothers of young children are expected to mirror those of Sweden in the 1970s.

Gender Differences. How do men and women who are parents fare in a society that explicitly values and promotes gender equality? Unlike the general (but by no means unanimous) consensus in Sweden, we in the United States agree far less about what men's and women's roles in society should be. But there is an undeniable drift towards greater sex-role convergence in all advanced countries, including the United States (e.g., Pleck, 1985; Robinson, 1985; Juster, 1985). As gender roles change, what policies and employment conditions seem best to facilitate the well-being of both men and women?

Social Class Differences. A critical marker of access to all types of resources in every society is location in the social structure. The systematic distribution of resources across different social categories of people has obvious sociological implications. Psychological well-being, like other, more tangible resources, is clearly related to socioeconomic status (Rainwater, 1974a,b; Hoffman, 1984). Socioeconomic position, defined generally in terms of one's social status and relation to the means of production, can serve as a proxy for a variety of family resources (e.g., education and skills, buying power, access to information). Location in the social structure (social class) is also a determinant of employment conditions and, through the impact of these conditions, of individual well-being.

Life Stage Variations. In one sense, life stage is held constant in this study, because I focus specifically on Swedish parents of preschoolers. But a cross-sectional portrait of this group would mask the fact that they are really quite diverse. Some, for example, have just become first-time parents, assuming that role with all its pleasures and responsibilities. Others are parents who have recently added a second or third child to their families. And still others are moving out of the childbearing stage, as their youngest child enters grade school. Each of these groups may encounter distinctive problems in managing work and family obligations.

Societal Differences. Although this study reports the findings of research in Sweden, in many ways it is also a book about the United States. No existing data source permits detailed comparisons between the two countries, but a comparative approach is nevertheless adopted wherever possible. Albeit to differing degrees, both countries face the reality of maternal employment. But Sweden has been in the forefront of social change in adopting policies to provide for the needs of working parents, whereas the United States is just beginning to give such policies serious consideration. For example, in 1985 a bill was introduced into the United States Congress for the first time mandating (unpaid) parental leaves of absence, whereas Sweden enacted legislation providing for such leaves for mothers as early as 1937 and for both parents in 1974.

For Swedish parents, the chief means of reconciling work and family life lie in the institutional supports created by legislative action in the 1970s. Given the kind of data available for Sweden, it is not possible to establish unequivocal linkages between changes in parental well-being and the expanded employment options this legislation made available to parents. Nevertheless, by documenting changes in both well-being and working conditions during the same time the study can, at the very least, contribute to more informed judgments about the effects of social policies explicitly aimed at lessening the burdens of employed parents.

The Swedish Level of Living Survey

The first Level of Living Survey was launched in 1968 with household interviews of 5923 randomly selected individuals aged 15–75. The same sample was reinterviewed in 1974, supplemented with new respondents in the younger age groups, and again in 1981 to monitor changes over time. The data are weighted to represent a total Swedish population in this age group of approximately six million people (Erikson and Åberg, 1987).

From this archive I selected all men and women respondents who reported having a child under age seven (when elementary school begins in Sweden) living with them at the time they were interviewed. The data are of two types: (1) those from comparable cross-sections of Swedish parents, used in a time-series fashion in order to assess general trends in working conditions and well-being; and (2) those from two cohorts of individual parents followed across the 1968–74 and the 1974–81 survey periods. These cohorts consist of Swedes who either were parents of preschoolers at the time of the first survey or became parents by the second survey period. Each of the cross-sectional subsamples (1968, 1974, 1981) is composed of approximately 1000 individuals. The 1968–74 cohort consists of 1463 parents, and the 1974–81 cohort contains 1397 parents.

These panel data offer an excellent opportunity to include time as a dimension of the analysis of changes in parents' circumstances. They permit the exploration of lagged effects—the possibility that the effects of particular conditions of work (or, for women, the act of entering the labor force) may manifest themselves only after a period of years. They enable us to examine not only change, but its equally revealing obverse, stability. How persistent, over time, are particular conditions or life strains? Without evidence such as that in the Level of Living Survey, we can only conjecture.

Standardized interviews of a representative population sample cannot, of course, fully illuminate the conditions of families with children. Many of the factors contributing to the well-being of children and their parents are too complex and subtle to be captured by structured questionnaires. But a sample survey such as the Level of Living Survey *can* provide an excellent starting point for estimating the prevalence of some of the principal problems encountered by parents and for determining the degree to which these are differently experienced by different groups (e.g., women in single-parent vs. two-parent households, employed mothers vs. employed fathers). A large-scale survey also can relate differences in the frequency and severity of problems people encounter to their location in the socioeconomic class structure.

To supplement the analysis of the Level of Living Survey data I have drawn upon the research literature to determine, as far as possible, how the experiences of Swedish parents compare with those of working parents in the United States. In addition, I have also used insights from more qualitative information gathered during a seven-month stay in Sweden in 1983 and a one-month stay in 1985, when I conducted informal interviews with a varied group of people in a number of institutional settings and more systematically interviewed thirty parents of preschoolers (a "purposive sample"). I found that how people described their lives conformed well to the statistical portrait produced from the survey data.

Scope of the Study

The main investigations of 'women's roles' need to be supplemented by studies of 'men's roles.' Or rather, the roles of both sexes should be considered. (Holter, 1970, p. 16)

After a discussion of social and theoretical contexts (Chapter 2) I consider, in the first half of the volume, issues of stability and change. Chapter 3 looks at the strains experienced by parents from 1968 to 1981. Are parents of young children in the early 1980s better or worse off than those in the late 1960s? How do the experiences of people who were parents in 1968 or had a child by 1974 compare with those of people who

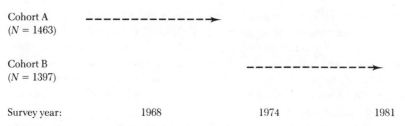

Figure 1.1. Sample size and survey years for two cohorts of Swedish parents of young children, that is, individuals who either had children under seven during the first survey period, or who became parents by the time of the second survey period.

were parents in 1974 or had a child by 1981? Each of these two groups is tracked through the next survey (to 1974 for the 1968–74 cohort and to 1981 for the 1974–81 cohort; see Figure 1.1) to examine well-being over time. I employ multivariate techniques to examine the links between various individual and family characteristics and the psychological health of parents.

Chapter 4 examines the working hours and working conditions of Swedish parents, looking also at gender and social class, to determine the extent to which their employment experiences have in fact changed from 1968 to 1981, a period during which a high political priority was assigned to improving the quality of working life.

The remainder of the volume looks for linkages between the two major sets of variables, working conditions—working hours, job demands, autonomy—and well-being. Because working conditions typically differ by gender, and because women and men have different family obligations, the models of well-being are estimated separately for men and women for each of the two cohorts studied.

Chapter 5 relates well-being to specific working conditions; Chapter 6 focuses on subgroups of parents: those from different social classes, and those who only recently became parents. I also investigate women who made the transition to motherhood under quite different conditions: those who reported high levels of psychological distress and fatigue before motherhood, and those with no such symptoms. How important is previous psychological history to subsequent well-being?

Why limit a study of the well-being of working parents to only those with young children in the home? Quite simply because existing theory and research establish that the early years of childbearing and child-rearing are the most crucial for the development of the child as well as the most stressful for parents (Aldous and Hill, 1969; Pearlin et al., 1981; Bronfenbrenner, 1979).

Why concentrate attention on the impact of employment conditions on well-being? First, because of the dramatic change that has taken place in the work roles of mothers of young children, and second, because employment is arguably the preeminent determinant of the time and energy available for parenting as well as a potent influence on self-esteem and overall well-being (Moore and Hofferth, 1979; Piotrkowski, 1979; Rapoport and Rapoport, 1975; Bohen and Viveros-Long, 1981; Pleck, 1985).

Significance

The goal of equality is to create a 'whole and indivisible human being.' . . . It all boils down to people's capacity to integrate private with public roles, roles in reproduction with roles in production. (Lilejström et al., 1978, p. 20)

The research reported in this book grows out of both scientific and social policy considerations. From a sociological perspective, it addresses work and family issues in a dynamic, systemic framework, illuminating the ways in which these two institutions relate to one another. Unlike most research on employment, which typically concentrates on individuals in their work roles, I focus on those who are *at the same time* workers and parents and who necessarily have interests and obligations that transcend their employment. In addition, I incorporate a more dynamic life course perspective than is customary in family research and in social research generally, examining stability and change over time rather than offering only single-frame "snapshots" at one point in time.

The study sheds badly needed light on a remarkable social transformation, one creating major changes in the character of the labor force, the definition of gender roles, and the nature of family life: the historically unprecedented increase in the labor force participation of mothers of young children. It is not yet clear how the consequent transformation in gender roles affects the psychological well-being of women or men. Although the employment of both parents outside the home is creating a major social quandary in virtually all industrialized countries, there has been surprisingly little systematic study of the interplay between women's (and, for that matter, men's) work and family lives. Because we don't understand the dimensions and ramifications of this issue, we do not know how best to assist workers who are also parents.

As other social scientists have pointed out (e.g., Coleman, 1986; Elder, 1974), even the most elegant theories of social change are of little value if they do not generate cogent explanations of how basic changes in social structure relate to changes in individual circumstances and behavior. The

Swedish labor market policies devised for working parents in the 1970s provide a "natural experiment" (Bronfenbrenner, 1979) of interest to all industrialized nations, in that it enables us to assess the effectiveness of a set of institutional supports created to aid employed parents in better meshing work and family roles.

2

The Social and Theoretical Context

Sweden: The Social Context

In Sweden they dreamed of being able to produce the good
human being by legislation; or more precisely, of legislating evil
out of existence. (Enquist, 1984, p. 63)

Why Sweden?
The working conditions and well-being of Swedish parents are the focus
of this study for four principal reasons. First, public debate regarding the
possible deleterious effects of employment on parenting has been
nowhere more spirited than in Sweden (e.g., Scott, 1982; NCE, 1979;
Wistrand, 1981; Ministry of Labor, 1985). One consequence was the
adoption in the 1970s of several imaginative legislative reforms, including paid parental leaves of absence, time off from work to take care of a
sick child, publicly supported day care, and the option of part-time
employment for parents of preschool children. The enactment of this
social legislation was expressly intended to alleviate the contradictions
and tensions between organizational obligations and family needs. These
family-related policies were not embraced wholeheartedly by all
Swedes. The trade unions, for example, originally opposed the part-time
employment option. Nevertheless, by now there is widespread acceptance of these parental supports throughout Sweden (Baude, 1983; Sundström, 1987; LO, 1987).

Sweden stands at the forefront of advanced industrialized societies in
its explicit recognition of the dilemmas of employed parents as a public
rather than a private issue and its adoption of a number of structural
reforms. At the same time, Swedish women also are in the vanguard of

15

social change, as is demonstrated by their wholesale entry into the labor force (discussed in more detail later). In these respects, Sweden offers a unique opportunity to examine the work–family nexus by analyzing changes in the psychological well-being of parents before and after the major influx of women into the labor force and the adoption of these legislative initiatives.

Second, Sweden has also enacted labor market legislation to provide protections against job and income loss. Although unemployment rates in Sweden are low compared to those in the United States (ranging from 1.5 to 2.7 percent in the 1970s, whereas the U.S. rate peaked at 8.5 percent in 1975; Ginsburg, 1983), joblessness has been an issue of continuous public concern, resulting in the adoption of an assortment of strategies to reduce both the incidence and the economic and human costs of unemployment. These include relief work, job placement assistance and training, and regional economic development.

Sweden has pursued this active labor market policy since the 1950s, but in the 1970s, in the face of an economic slowdown and relatively high unemployment, a number of new measures reemphasized the long-established goal of full employment. The Promotion of Employment Act of 1974 required that County Labor Market Boards be notified at least two months before impending layoffs. The Security of Employment Act, also enacted in 1974, required that employees be given from one to six months (depending on seniority) advance notice before any planned layoff. And the Codetermination Act, first implemented in 1977, required that employers not make personnel cuts without prior negotiations with their employees' unions (Swedish Institute, 1983; Ginsburg, 1983).

The full import of these policies for parents of young children, a group historically vulnerable to job loss and insecurity (Moen et al., 1983), has yet to be determined. Leighton and Gustafsson (1984) have documented shifts in the distribution of joblessness that augur to the disadvantage of women while reducing risks to prime-age males. They suggest that an increase in the numbers of temporary workers (in many cases hired to fill in for those on parental leaves) may well mean that for a significant portion of the labor force employment insecurity, rather than security, is the norm. The present study examines this possibility by documenting the prevalence and distribution by gender of unemployment and temporary employment among parents located in different strata of the occupational hierarchy (see Chapter 4).

Third, Sweden is commonly regarded as a world leader in efforts to create work environments more conducive to meeting employee needs. In particular, the Codetermination Act of 1977 and the Work Environment Act of 1978 widened protection of workers' safety and health

(Swedish Institute, 1983). Health, in the Swedish perspective, is broadly defined to include mental and social as well as physical well-being (Levi, 1978). Thus, legislation designed to improve the work environment addresses such issues as psychological stress, monotony, and the organization of work. Greater worker autonomy is also a goal of the Work Environment statute, which states that "work should be arranged so that the worker can influence his or her work situation" (MacLeod, 1984, p. 7). What remains to be seen is how the resultant improvements in working conditions are distributed across various subgroups of Swedish parents and which specific conditions of work most affect individual well-being.

Finally, Sweden, as the pace-setter in confronting the changing nature of men's and women's roles, offers a natural "laboratory" in which to examine issues and options that will inevitably come to the fore in the United States in the 1990s, as the proportion of American mothers in the labor force approaches that of Sweden. For example, the United States Bureau of Labor Statistics estimates that by 1995 the labor force participation rate of women in their twenties and early thirties—the child-bearing years—will reach 80 percent, which was the rate for Swedish mothers of preschoolers in 1981 (Women's Bureau, 1985). By 1990 nearly half of the American labor force will be female, and over 80 percent of these women are expected to become pregnant at sometime during their working lives (Bohen, 1983).

A Postindustrial Society

Welfare ideology seeks rational, predictable solutions to man's tribulations. To meet the demands for justice and equality of that ideology, rational humanitarianism must be meted out on a predetermined impersonal basis . . . the milk of human kindness therefore flows less frequently from one human being to another; instead, it is dispensed in homogenized form through regulations and institutions. (Zetterberg, 1984, pp. 90–91)

The term "postindustrial society" is often used loosely to characterize highly developed countries in the Western world. Sociologists and economists append various texts to this rubric, but most often describe countries marked by the ascendancy of the service sector, with attendant economic, technological, and social changes that transform the character of contemporary life. Among these transformations are a declining fertility rate, fewer external or normative constraints on life styles (e.g., whether to marry, to have children, to move), a progressive shift toward public provision of what were formerly private services (such as care for the aged or young), and narrowing differences in gender roles at every stage of the life course.

Demographic Change. Sweden is commonly seen as the epitome of postindustrialization. For example, the fertility rate is extremely low—in 1983, 1.6 children for each woman in the childbearing years, compared to a U.S. rate of 1.8 per woman (Boethius, 1984; U.S. Bureau of the Census, 1986). Most Swedish women have only one or two children; only 2 percent of the families with children have as many as four, compared to 12 percent in the United States (U.S. Bureau of the Census, 1984). But demographers Hoem and Hoem (1987) describe the progression to second births in Sweden as "steady and unabated" (p. 3), and indeed, estimate the rate in 1987 to be 1.85; there has been no trend toward permanent childlessness or the one-child family.

As in the United States, the low birth rate in Sweden means, among other things, that the population is progressively aging. Moreover, as in all industrialized countries, average life expectancy has increased dramatically—in 1983 to eighty years for women and seventy-four years for men (Statistics Sweden, 1985). By 1984 about 17 percent of the Swedish population was over sixty-five years old, compared to 12 percent of the U.S. population (U.S. Bureau of the Census, 1984).

The average age of first marriage also has increased, from 23.6 years for women and 26.0 years for men in 1970 to 26.6 and 29.2 years, respectively, in 1982 (Statistics Sweden, 1982). The corresponding age at first marriage for American women in 1982 was 22.5 years, the highest since 1890; and for American men it was 25.1 years, the highest since 1910 (Espenshade, 1985).

Marriage itself has become more optional than the traditional expectation. Cohabitation became increasingly popular in the 1970s, especially for younger couples (Hoem and Hoem, 1987; Tröst, 1985). Although it is difficult to measure the prevalence of nonmarital cohabitation, it is estimated that close to one in four Swedish couples living together are not married, compared to an estimated one in twenty in the United States (Etzler, 1987; Popenoe, 1987). Government policies and legislation have blurred the once sharp distinctions between marriage and cohabitation in Sweden, making cohabitation "legally and culturally . . . an accepted alternative rather than a prelude to marriage" (Popenoe, 1987, p. 176).

Moreover, having a child is no longer an incentive to marriage, as witnessed by the high rates of Swedish children (45 percent in 1984) born out of wedlock (compared to 18 percent in the United States; U.S. Bureau of the Census, 1986). This in itself marks a rapid social change; in 1970 only 18 percent of all Swedish children were born outside marriage (the 1970 U.S. rate was 10.7; Espenshade, 1985). But although almost half of all

Swedish children are born out of wedlock "nearly all of them are born to parents who live together in a marital or nonmarital union" (Hoem and Hoem, 1987, p. 3). These cohabiting parents are typically in a stable relationship with many of the legal rights and obligations of a marriage (Ekdahl, 1984; Hoem and Hoem, 1987).

But dissolution rates—high for married couples—are estimated to be as much as three times higher for cohabiting couples (Popenoe, 1987). Hoem and Hoem (1987) point out, "it is part of the purpose of early nonmarital cohabitation that it should entail looser bonds than a legal marriage, and indeed, consensual unions break up more easily than marriages" (p. 12). This, in conjunction with the high divorce rates in Sweden, means that significant numbers of children live with only one parent. Almost one in five (18 percent) Swedish households with children is headed by a single parent, a proportion comparable to that (21.5 percent) in the United States.

In short, neither love and marriage nor parenthood and marriage necessarily go together. Bernhardt (1987a) summarizes the Swedish scene, "we have a new pattern of male-female interaction, characterized by an increasing prevalence of informal cohabitation rather than formalized marriage, increasing dissolution rates and a lessening economic dependence on the part of the woman in a partner relationship" (p. 27).

Gender Role Change. The increasing convergence of men's and women's roles is most manifest in the movement of women into the labor force. More than two-thirds (67.9 percent) of Swedish women aged 17–64 were in the labor force in 1975, compared to just under half (49.0 percent) of women in this age group in the United States (Women's Bureau, 1985). By 1984 the Swedish labor force participation rate of women aged 17–64 had risen to 78 percent (Ministry of Labor, 1985); the U.S. rate was 65.1 percent for this age group in March, 1986 (Paul O. Flaim, BLS, personal communication, August 1987). The greatest change in both countries has been in the employment of women with preschool children: 86 percent of Swedish mothers of young children were in the labor force in 1986, compared to 54.4 percent of American mothers of preschoolers (Sundström, 1987; Paul O. Flaim, BLS, personal communication, August 1987).

By 1985, 47 percent of the Swedish labor force was female, and by the end of the 1980s the female labor force participation rate is expected to equal that of men (Gustafsson, 1984a). In the United States a similar increase is also likely to occur, but at a much slower pace; women now constitute 44 percent of the labor force, and married women's labor force participation is expected to approximate that of married men by the year 2000 (Davis, 1984).

Large numbers of Swedish women, however, work less than full-time. In 1986, 45.3 percent of those employed worked fewer than 35 hours per week, down from a high of 56.5 percent in 1982 (Sundström, 1987; the comparable proportion of American women in 1984 was 27 percent— Women's Bureau, 1985). But in Sweden, part-time work is not categorically different from full-time work: part-timers who work at least 17 hours a week receive the same, or a prorated share of, benefits accorded to full-time employees, and all employees, regardless of hours worked, are entitled to vacations, sick leave, and retirement benefits. This stands in marked contrast to part-time employment in the United States, much of which is concentrated in low-level and low-paying jobs offering neither security nor basic fringe benefits.

Nevertheless, this restricted labor force involvement of Swedish women, especially mothers, reflects something of a discrepancy between national ideology concerning gender equality and the reality of Swedish life. Swedish women, like their U.S. counterparts, continue to perform the bulk of the household chores (Bernhardt, 1987a; Haas, 1982; Wistrand, 1981; Fritzell, 1985; Sandqvist, 1987a,b; Sundström, 1987). Even in advanced industrialized societies, there remains "homework" to be done: "to take care of the children, to shop, to prepare the meals, to see that the clothes are clean and mended and that the home is tidy—all these are chores which to a large extent still are performed in private homes" (Boalt, quoted in Sundström, 1987, p. 120). The distribution of housework among Swedish couples in 1975 (Figure 2.1) is very probably much the same today. Men's family "work" by no means approaches the time women spend in domestic activities. A 1984 Swedish study found that fathers of children under five spend an average of 7 hours a week in basic child care, mothers 16.5 hours. Additionally, fathers spend 0.8 of an hour and mothers 2 hours in transporting children (Konsumentverket, 1984, cited in Sandqvist, 1987b).

But at least some Swedish fathers are putting more time into childcare (Haas, 1982). A (1984) study of a sample of parents of preschoolers found that where both parents work full time fathers are close to taking an equal share in "food-related work" and "general responsibility for children" (Sandqvist, 1987b, p. 189). Similarly, analysis of time-use data in the United States reveals

a marked shift in the distribution of work activity between men and women over the 75–76 to 81–82 period, that the proportion of time spent working for pay and working in the home has moved toward greater equality between the sexes, and that this pattern is most evident in the younger age groups (Juster, 1985, p. 318).

Swedish concern about the continuing inequalities between men and women led in 1983 to the creation of a study commission called the

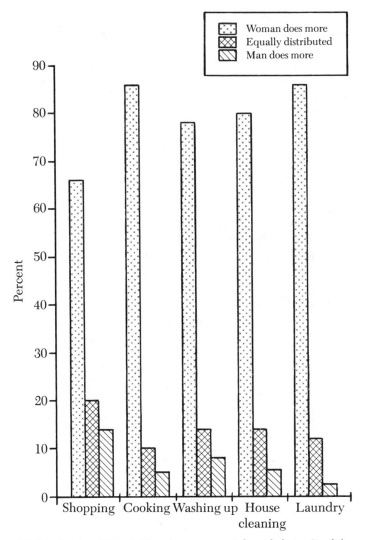

Figure 2.1. Distribution of household work among married or cohabiting Swedish couples, 1975. Source: Holland, 1980, p. vii.

"Working Party for the Role of the Male." Its chairman, Stig Ahs, makes the point that "we men are the prisoners of a system for which we ourselves are primarily responsible. A system that is not only detrimental to us as men but also postulates a role for women that renders any equality between the sexes impossible. Our male role makes us both oppressors and oppressed" (Ministry of Labor, 1986, p. 2). The commission concluded that becoming a parent is one of several watersheds in men's lives offering opportunities for transcending traditional gender role behavior. Still more pointedly, the Swedish Marriage Act, effective in January, 1986, states that "spouses shall jointly care for the home and the children and promote the well-being of the family on the basis of joint consultation."

This legislative language cannot mask the persistent shortfall in gender equality, in marriage as elsewhere in Swedish society. But these disparities between ideology and achievement are often papered over by both men and women. Thus, Haavind asserts that there are now in Sweden new rules for the old gender game: "A woman is positively judged as feminine according to her capacity to have male dominance look like something else—something she wants, something caused by necessity or practical reasons or something caused by love" (quoted in Bernhardt, 1987a, p. 28). And Jalmert has coined the phrase "the in-principle man" to describe those men who agree in principle that they should share domestic burdens but feel it is not practical in their case (Sandqvist, 1987b, p. 36).

Changes in the Economy. As gauged by its economic structure, Sweden is well in the midst of a postindustrial period. Only 30 percent of the Swedish labor force works in the mining, manufacturing, and construction industries, whereas 52 percent is located in the private and public service sectors (see Figure 2.2). In fact, the number of public employees at the local government level doubled between 1970 and 1982, so that they are nearly as numerous as workers in industrial jobs (Swedish Institute, 1983). By 1984 almost one in three (32 percent) Swedish workers was employed in the public service sector (Lapping, 1987). The United States labor force has also undergone dramatic changes: only 25 percent are now employed in industrial occupations and 72 percent in service, transportation, or trade industries; 16 percent are in the public sector (derived from Women's Bureau, 1986).

Although 90 percent of its companies are privately owned, Sweden is often depicted as a "socialist" country. This label more accurately refers not to its economic system but to its comprehensive social welfare system, which provides general social insurance, child allowances, free education, and guaranteed health care for all permanent residents. In addition to these entitlements, housing allowances are granted to all families in need. In 1981, about one-third of Swedish households with children under age seventeen received housing support (Kindlund, 1984). Although the term "welfare state" has a negative connotation to many in the United States, conjuring up visions of cradle-to-grave dependence on government, in Sweden the image is far more positive. The aim is to pro-

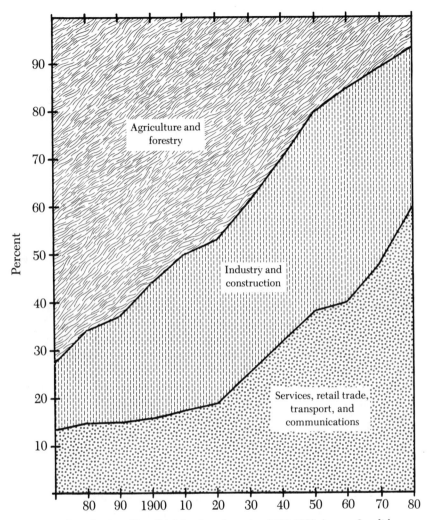

Figure 2.2. Distribution of Swedish labor force by sector, 1870–1980. Source: Swedish Institute, 1984, p. 45.

mote individual and family well-being by establishing a more equitable distribution of resources concomitant with a progressively higher standard of living (Hadenius, 1985).

One transformation characteristic of advanced industrial societies and particularly true of Sweden is the shift of caretaking activities from the home to the public sector. Much of what typically was women's unpaid work—such as caring for the young, the old, the sick—remains work performed by women, but it now takes the form of jobs in the service sector (Haavio-Mannila and Kari, 1980).

The less favorable aspect of this picture of comprehensive care and security is the high tax rate required to finance social welfare programs. A typical full-time worker pays 30–40 percent of his or her income in direct taxes. Although families with children do benefit from certain tax concessions to help compensate for childcare costs, the marginal tax rate in Sweden remains quite high by American standards.

Labor Market Legislation and Family Policies in the 1970s

Swedes became used to the idea that social policies, to be effective, cannot be applied individually, like band aids or the legendary finger in the dike, but must be part of a consistent program. (Scott, 1982, p. 1)

Most pertinent to the lives and well-being of parents of young children are the labor market and family policies that were either initiated or elaborated during the 1970s. These addressed two sets of issues that are particularly germane to working parents: those of equality between men and women and those aimed at reducing the strains of employment.

Equality Between Men and Women. The last two decades have seen enormous strides in the promotion of equality between the sexes in Sweden. Although the principal legislation, an "Act on Equality Between Men and Women At Work," was not passed until 1980, the equality theme permeated the 1970s and is best expressed in a 1968 report to the United Nations: "Every individual irrespective of sex shall have the same practical opportunities not only for education or employment but also in principle the same responsibility for his or her own maintenance as well as shared responsibility for the upbringing of children and the upkeep of the home" (Scott, 1982, p. 3). With this pronouncement Sweden became, in 1968, the first country to adopt a policy of sex-role equality geared to altering the roles of men as well as women. The legislative steps initiated in the 1970s must be viewed, then, as part of a deliberate strategy to recast the lives of Swedish citizens.

The Act on Equality expressly prohibits discrimination by sex in hiring, promoting, and training workers, and it encourages affirmative action in placing men and women in positions that are nontraditional for their sex. This act addresses the very issues that dominated formal and informal discussions in the 1970s regarding the sexual division of roles in the home and in society generally (NCE, 1979; Wistrand, 1981; Scott, 1982).

Basic to an understanding of the transformations in gender roles in the

1970s are the changes made in the Swedish tax system. An option of separate taxation for husbands and wives initiated in 1967 was made mandatory by 1971. This reform helped implement the policy that every adult—male or female—should be economically independent and responsible for his or her own support (Scott, 1982). Swedish income tax is steeply progressive, with a top marginal rate of 80 percent. Thus it is financially more advantageous for two parents to work than for one of them to earn their combined wages by working their total combined hours. This system of progressive individual rather than family taxation provided a strong incentive for women who were wives and mothers to enter and remain in the labor force, and helped spur the dramatic increase in women's employment during the 1970s.

Supports for Parents. Particularly vital to the reconciliation of work and family roles is the system of parental insurance that was established in 1974 as an outgrowth of the maternity leave arrangements then in effect. This insurance permitted either the father or the mother to take six months of paid leave of absence upon the birth of a child and to receive, typically, 90 percent of the normal wage. The parental leave benefit is paid for by the Riksforsakringsverket (Social Insurance Board) rather than by employers directly. To qualify, workers had only to be employed for nine months prior to the child's birth.[1] In 1978 this benefit was expanded to permit either parent to stay home for an additional 180 working days, with 90 percent of their income for the first three months and a small standard benefit rate thereafter. In 1980 parents received 90 percent of their wages for nine out of twelve months of leave. After 1980, employed parents could also extend their leave of absence, by combining paid and unpaid leaves, for up to eighteen months following the birth of a child.

In addition to parental leave, an expectant mother is entitled to a pregnancy benefit which allows her to take paid time off during the later stage of her pregnancy if the nature of her work prevents her from continuing her regular employment and if a transfer to other duties is not possible. In addition, fathers are entitled to ten days off, with compensation, in connection with childbirth in order to assist in caring for the new mother and infant as well as other children at home.

As already noted, the 1974 Act was preceded by a number of earlier maternity benefits (see Table 2.1). But what is particularly unique about this legislation is its provision of benefits to both parents rather than mothers alone.

1. Women not in the labor force also receive a small payment after childbearing, but the amount is limited.

Table 2.1. Work–family policies in Sweden

1937	Maternity benefits passed
1939	Abolished worker discrimination on the basis of pregnancy
1947	Child allowance introduced
1971	Separate income tax assessment for husband and wife
1974	Parental insurance entitling both mother and father to share paid leave of absence after birth of child
1978	Paid leave extended to 270 days
1979	Parents of infants entitled to six-hour days
1980	Paid leave extended to 360 days and "sick" leave for temporary care of children increased to 60 days

Source: Statistics Sweden, March 1985.

Still another benefit provided by this legislation is the right of parents to stay home to care for sick children. In 1977 this provision was expanded to allow parents to remain home when the normal caretaker for the child was ill. By 1980 parents were able to take up to sixty days of such paid leave per year per child, although in practice the average in 1984 was seven days, about equally divided between fathers and mothers (Ministry of Labor, 1985).

By 1984, 85 percent of fathers were also taking advantage of the ten-day childbirth-related benefit, staying home an average of eight days following the birth of their child. But comparatively few were participating in the parental leave program: only one in five had taken a portion of the parental leave, staying home on average about forty-one days (NCE, 1985). By 1986 this had risen to only 27 percent (Haas, 1987). Nonetheless, these numbers are significantly greater than the 2 percent of fathers who took leave in 1975. Swedish fathers are more likely to take parental leaves if they are in public sector jobs and have women coworkers. Some men do not take such leaves for fear they might be ridiculed by their colleagues (Haas, 1987; Ministry of Labor, 1986; Sandqvist, 1987a).

A second important parental support was legislatively established in 1979, giving parents of children under age eight the right to reduce their working time to six hours a day with a proportional reduction in wages. (Workers in the public sector had such an option long before this 1979 law was enacted.) Mothers have typically been the ones to take advantage of this reduced-time employment opportunity: fully two-thirds of all mothers of preschoolers have become part-time workers (Bernhardt, 1987a,b; Sundström, 1987).

A third basic support for working parents is the provision of childcare assistance. Five different arrangements are available: (1) day nurseries (typically open from 6:30 A.M. to 6:30 P.M. and caring for children from six months to seven years of age), (2) part-time groups (three hours of activities for six-year olds and, when space is available, five-year-olds), (3) recreation centers (providing before- and after-school care for children aged seven to twelve), (4) small home day-nurseries (offering family day care for up to four children and paid for by the local government), and (5) open preschools which enable nonemployed parents and children to meet together under trained leadership. The responsibility for these childcare programs is assigned to the local government, and they are located in residential neighborhoods.

The first legislation of preschool programs went into effect in 1975, calling for greatly expanded day care facilities. By 1983, about 44 percent of Swedish children under age seven were cared for by a parent at home; 38 percent were in government-sponsored childcare facilities (17 percent in day care centers and 13 percent in family day nurseries) (Swedish Institute, 1984; Statistics Sweden, 1985; see Figure 2.3). Of children who had both parents employed in 1983, almost a fourth (24 percent) were cared for by a parent at home, and more than half (55 percent) were enrolled in municipal day care facilities (Statistics Sweden, 1985). But although the capacity of Swedish childcare facilities increased fourfold between 1968 and 1984 (Gustafsson, 1984), it remains insufficient to meet the demand. In response to this shortfall, the Swedish legislature mandated in 1985 that public childcare facilities be expanded by 1991 to meet the needs of all children over eighteen months old.

Fully comparable statistics for preschool children in the United States

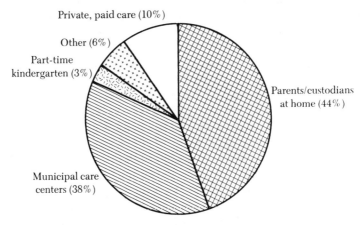

Figure 2.3. Who cares for children in Sweden, 1983. Children from ages 0–6 years are included. Virtually all children below 1 year are at home. All 6-year-olds and in some cases 5-year-olds are entitled to part-time kindergarten (up to 15 hours/week). Source: Statistics Sweden, 1985.

are not available. However, we do know that nearly half of the children of working women under age five in 1982 were cared for in someone else's home; less than a fifth (18 percent) were in a group care facility (U.S. Bureau of the Census, 1983). "Preschooler" in the United States is defined as a child under six, meaning that all six-year-olds are in school for a full school day. Almost all U.S. five-year-olds are in kindergarten or primary school, and more than half of those with working mothers are enrolled in a full school-day program. Moreover, over half of the four-year-olds with employed mothers are in at least a part-day preschool program. Still, the childcare provisions for employed parents in the United States are makeshift at best. The last major childcare bill in the United States passed Congress in 1971 but was vetoed by President Richard Nixon, who saw it as harmful to families. For Swedes, by contrast, it is the absence of adequate childcare that is viewed as harmful.

Public Strategies of Innovation and Response

We probably do not have better ideas, programmes or visions
within the labour movement in Sweden than in many other
countries, but we have an organization that many others lack.
(Arne Geijer, former President of Confederation of Trade Unions
cited in AIC, 1981, p. 3)

Government, management, and labor in Sweden have commonly acknowledged the possible deleterious effects of work life on parenting. A case in point is an "Agreement on Equality" proposed jointly by the Swedish Trade Union Confederation (Landsorganisationen i Svergi, LO), to which about 90 percent of blue-collar workers belong, and the employers' confederation (Svenska Arbetsgivareforengingen, SAF), whose members account for about 80 percent of private-sector employment: "The conditions of work shall be so arranged that they enable both men and women to combine a job outside the home with responsibility for a family" (LO, 1983). This statement clearly reflects both a shared commitment to gender equality and a common understanding of the importance, from a societal perspective, of investing time and money in children's care (Scott, 1982; Ministry of Labor, 1985, 1986).

Why is Sweden in the vanguard in addressing the dilemmas of working parents? Certainly this is a question for which there is no simple answer. But Sweden's small size (population of just over eight million) and its cultural homogeneity have facilitated the development of a consensus on national values and societal objectives.

One value—and an enduring one—is a strong concern for the social welfare of all citizens. Attention in Sweden has not been on women's rights per se but on human rights, not only on gender equality but on equality across all population groups, defined by class as well as gender. As Ruggie (1984) maintains, "perhaps the most significant development concerning women workers in Sweden is the tendency toward 'universalization' of the category of worker. This means that the distinctions among workers based on class, occupation, and sex are breaking down and becoming less determinant of worker's opportunities and rewards" (p. 340). For example, labor's "solidaristic wage policy," aimed at reducing income differentials by raising the wages of the lowest paid, has been an important component of the larger effort to reduce inequality in Swedish society. The trade unions (LO) have historically bargained for higher wages among the poorly paid (Korpi, 1974). One consequence of this successful campaign has been to narrow the gap between men's and women's wages in spite of the continuing occupational segregation by gender. On average, working women in Sweden in 1985 earned over 80 percent of working men's wages, compared to only 69 percent in the United States in 1988 (Ministry of Labor, 1985; Paul O. Flaim, BLS, May 1988).

Another factor contributing to Sweden's policy initiatives in the work–family domain is the prevailing view of the role of government in society. Because of Sweden's strong and influential labor movement, with its political as well as collective bargaining arms, government is generally regarded as a constructive instrument of social change rather than as an intrusive and constraining force. The Social Democratic Party, which is closely allied with the principal trade union confederation, LO, enjoyed forty-four years of uninterrupted power in Sweden, from 1932 to 1976. For a brief four years, a nonsocialist coalition (of Center, Conservative, and Liberal parties) assumed the reins of government, only to lose control in 1979 when the Social Democrats again took power (Hadenius, 1985).

The Social Democrats have long championed economic security, creating a multifaceted social insurance system to provide for the basic needs of all Swedish citizens. The family policies of paid parental leave and time off for childcare are integral components of this system. These benefits have also been important for a stable labor force. Ruggie (1984) suggests that "the key to the changes that have occurred in Swedish policies for working women is the close association between concern for women, the labor market, and economic productivity. Women's concerns . . . are placed within the main stream of economic policy" (p. 297). Consequently, from the perspective of both social welfare and economic productivity these policies for working parents are regarded as essential to enhance the overall quality of life in Sweden—apart from the more specific aim of promoting equal opportunities for men and women.

A U.S. Comparison. In the United States, a national family or child-care policy is yet to be adopted. Nor is there a general consensus about the roles of men and women or of government in the care and upbringing of children. Indeed, Kamerman and Kahn (1981) suggest that the failure to confront the problems of workers with family responsibilities may well be a way of avoiding emotionally charged and potentially divisive issues of maternal employment and family structure.

Thus far the principal legislation in the United States affecting working parents is the Pregnancy Discrimination Act of 1978, which prohibits discrimination in employment on the basis of pregnancy, childbirth, or related medical conditions. Because this act requires that women so affected "be treated the same for all employment-related purposes" as other employees, disability benefits (usually amounting to a paid six weeks leave) must be provided to women at the time of childbirth, if they are covered by disability insurance. Unfortunately, only about 40 percent of all working women live in states providing such coverage. Maternity or parental leave is not a federally mandated employment benefit and is granted at the discretion of employers. It was estimated that in 1978 a six weeks paid leave for childbirth was available to fewer than a third of all employed women (Kamerman et al., 1983). A more recent study of Fortune 1500 companies found that slightly over half offered some unpaid leave for women and fewer than two-fifths offer some unpaid paternity leave (Catalyst, 1986). Unfortunately, however, only a minority of employed women work in such large corporations.

A landmark bill providing unpaid parental leave was introduced into both houses of Congress in 1985. If enacted, the bill (the Parental and Disability Leave Act of 1985) would have provided workers up to 26 weeks of unpaid medical leave and 18 weeks of unpaid leave for the care of a newborn, newly adopted, or seriously ill child, with guaranteed reinstatement rights. A compromise bill, providing for reduced benefits and coverage, was subsequently reported favorably out of the House Education and Labor Committee in 1987. However, though widely supported by women's, children's, and family advocacy groups, as well as by organized labor, the Family and Medical Leave Act of 1987 was strenuously opposed by the business community, particularly the National Association of Manufacturers and the Chamber of Commerce, and by the Reagan Administration.

Still, the fact that the level and intensity of debate about work and family issues are increasing in both private and public arenas in the United States suggests that governments, employers, and organized labor are coming to view the problems of working parents as more than the private troubles of individual families (see, e.g., Bohen, 1983; Fernandez, 1985; Friedman, 1986; Axel, 1985; Statuto, 1984; Gladstone et al., 1985). Although there has been little progress in adopting public policies to aid working parents, a growing number of private and public sector employers have begun to address the needs of the changing work force by providing various kinds of childcare assistance (most commonly information and referral services), flexible work schedules, limited maternity and parental leaves (though typically without pay), opportunities for reduced working hours, and, on occasion, work sharing and work at home (Axel, 1985). In examining experience to date, however, it is clear that the work-family and gender role issues that rose to prominence on the Swedish national agenda in the 1970s are only now being joined in the United States.

Theoretical Context

Interconnections between Work and Family

To the extent that as sociologists we are interested in ordinary
people representative of major population groups rather than in
exotic and extraordinary individuals. . . . attention to social
roles and the strains experienced within them serves us well.
Clearly, it is around daily and enduring roles such as breadwinning and work or marriage and parenthood that much of our
lives are structured through time. It is here that researchers are
most likely to find the seedbeds of stress. (Pearlin, 1983, p. 5)

Traditionally, studies of work and occupations have focused almost exclusively on the individual only as a worker, neglecting the fact that he (and commonly the worker is seen as male) typically and concurrently functions as a member of a family unit. Those who have recognized the essential intertwining of work life and life outside work have generally subscribed to either a compensatory or a spillover interpretation of work–nonwork relationships (Wilensky, 1960). The compensatory view holds that experiences outside work, including family life, tend to make up for the deficits of employment. Workers whose needs and aspirations are thwarted on the job gravitate toward activities off the job which offset this deprivation. This is the view held by those who describe the family as a refuge from the outside world (Lasch, 1977; Zaretsky, 1976). The second perspective, which is best supported by observation and research and which guides the research reported here, argues that employment experience, whether positive or negative, overflows the boundaries of the workplace and permeates the whole of life, including the family (Kornhauser, 1965; Gardell, 1976; Kohn, 1980; Kohn and Schooler, 1983; Piotrkowski, 1975).

A Life Course Perspective

The years between 25 and 35 are the prime years for establishing
a successful career. These are the years when hard work has the
maximum payoff. They are also the prime years for launching a
family. Women who leave the job market completely during
those years may find that they never catch up. (Thurow, 1984)

The life course perspective attends to the intersections of the multiple
strands that go to make up the individual's life—the relationship, for
example, between parenting and career development. Because of the
interdependence and timing of work and family roles, researchers identify the years of parenthood as a typically stressful period for young
adults (e.g., Rossi, 1968). The problem in early adulthood is not being a
parent per se or working per se, but synchronizing the two. It may not be
the transition to parenthood that is most commonly the source of stress
but the day-to-day, relatively fixed and enduring strains of establishing
oneself occupationally while simultaneously raising a family (Pearlin,
1980, 1983; Pearlin and Lieberman, 1977).

Parents of young children are not equally vulnerable to psychological
distress. But given that the early childrearing years are typically a
stressful life stage, how do some parents successfully avoid succumbing to
these strains? The life-course approach suggests that four factors need to
be taken into account:

1. *The Nature of the Job.* The organization and conditions of work have
   been shown to be directly related to the mental as well as the physical
   health of workers (Levi et al., 1982; Levi, 1974; Kahn, 1981; Katz and
   Kahn, 1978; Karasek, 1979, 1981; Miller et al., 1979). Parents who
   occupy psychologically and physically demanding jobs are, understandably, more likely to experience strains than are those whose
   occupations are less hectic, monotonous, or exhausting. But some features of jobs can enhance the well-being of parents. For example, jobs
   offering substantial discretion and opportunity for individual control
   over working hours may well preclude or at least reduce some of the
   role conflicts so commonly experienced by employed parents.
2. *The Nature of the Family.* Clearly, single parents are more vulnerable
   to role overloads and strains than are those who share family responsibilities with a spouse or partner (Cherlin, 1981). Similarly, new and
   inexperienced parents and those with a number of children can be
   more prone to psychological distress (Russell, 1974; Radloff, 1975;
   Belsky et al., 1984).
3. *Available Resources.* The more personal resources individuals bring to
   the early years of parenting the more likely they are to experience

higher levels of well-being. These resources include education and health as well as previous levels of well-being (Brown and Harris, 1978).

4. *Modes of Adaptation.* Swedish parents are fortunate to have a number of strategies available to them to lessen the stress of simultaneously managing work and family roles. Part-time employment and parental leaves of absence, for example, can be expected to reduce the strains experienced by working parents and, consequently, to enhance their well-being.

Job and Gender Models

Although each of the above factors may affect the well-being of parents, researchers seldom consider them in toto in their studies of men and women. Instead, investigators of psychological well-being typically employ the job and gender models described by Feldberg and Glenn (1979), concentrating on family factors when studying women and work factors when studying men. Women's psychological problems are seen as originating primarily in their family or household roles and relationships, and even if their labor force *participation* is taken into account, the specific *conditions* of their employment tend to be ignored.[2] Conversely, studies of men almost invariably focus on the work role, identifying features of the job situation which underlie good or poor mental health or relate to reported symptoms of distress. Men's family conditions are seldom considered (e.g., Karasek, 1979; Kohn and Schooler, 1983).

What is required, of course, is an approach that attends simultaneously to the family and work situations of both men and women. This is especially important since the employment conditions of men and women are likely to be quite dissimilar. Because of continued occupational segregation, even in Sweden, both the demands and the flexibility of women's and men's work situations may differ markedly.

Well-Being

People do not play roles in quite the way that the implied analogy to theater conveys. We play roles, but our roles also enter— and alter—our selves. (Veroff et al., 1981, p. 18)

Psychological well-being is far easier to discuss than to measure. As noted in Chapter 1, most scholars resort to measuring the absence of well-being

2. Examples of such studies using the gender model include Brown and Harris, 1978; Welch and Booth, 1977; Radloff, 1975; Wright, 1978; and Ferree, 1976. For a different approach using both job and gender models see Miller et al., 1979.

or subjective distress, often construed as some form of "unpleasant arousal," and including such symptoms as depression, anxiety, or sleeplessness (Thoits, 1983, p. 34). But this "dysphoric affect" is really a consequence of psychosocial stress, which can be defined any number of ways, from "the experience of unfulfilled need" (Kaplan, 1983, p. 196) to a "mismatch—actual or perceived—between the person and his or her environment" (Menaghan, 1983, p. 158). Working parents are positioned so as to be particularly susceptible to just such a mismatch. In attempting to reconcile the daily cross-pressures of work and family roles, they are most vulnerable to role strain, to "the hardships, challenges, and conflicts or other problems that people come to experience as they engage over time in normal social roles" (Pearlin, 1983, p. 8).

How can we measure the effects of these cross-pressures on the well-being of Swedish parents and, equally important, on *changes* in their well-being? Most studies treat well-being as a static phenomenon, something an individual either has or does not have at a particular time. But we all know from personal experience and from our own observations that well-being is fluid rather than constant. Ideally, then, we should measure its stability and change over time.

Like most comparable social surveys, the Level of Living Survey includes an inventory of various psychological symptoms, with a scale measuring their frequency over the past 12 months.[3] Despite their limitations, these subjective distress scales are useful, not so much as measures of mental impairment but as indicators of subjective dispositions, of how individuals in different statuses gauge their own mental health at given times and under different conditions (Veroff et al., 1981).

In addition to the checklist of psychosomatic symptoms I employ four other measures of well-being from the Level of Living Survey: (1) the absence of feelings of daily fatigue over the last two weeks, (2) feelings of physical exhaustion at the end of the working day, (3) feelings of psychological exhaustion at the end of the working day, and, for the 1981 interview, (4) subjective evaluations of life conditions (see Appendix A).

What is it in the backgrounds and experiences of parents that causes them to have different scores on these measures, and why do these scores change for some between surveys but not for others? Answering these

3. The items in this measure are listed in Appendix A. They are similar to those in use in the PERI Psychophysiologic Symptoms scale (Dohrenwend et al., 1981), the Center for Epidemiological Studies of Depression Scale (CES-D; Radloff, 1975, 1977), and the Macmillan Scale (Macmillan, 1957; Thoits and Hannan, 1979). Reporting few of the symptoms on the distress scale is certainly suggestive of individual well-being. Moreover, such a symptom scale offers an opportunity to examine general well-being across different social groups and at different historical periods.

questions directs attention to the roles people occupy in society and the conditions under which they perform these roles. Thus, these measures should permit us to determine how well-being is distributed among parents by gender and by their location in the social structure, and how it varies over time.

Employed Mothers

Fairness is not necessarily achieved by treating people who are
different as if they were just alike. (Davis and van den Oever,
1982, p. 510)

While the nature of the labor force changes as a function of growing maternal employment, family life is also undergoing a corresponding shift in organization and definition. Marriages are being transformed from a complementary relationship, in which husband and wife perform different but interdependent tasks, to a parallel relationship in which both spouses are employed and both share the domestic responsibilities for home and children. Domestic role-sharing is thus far limited; some see that as a cultural lag that in time will disappear (Ross, Mirowsky, and Huber, 1983). Changes in family roles undergird still more pervasive changes in societal attitudes regarding the proper roles of men and women. These trends in the labor force, in family life, and in gender-role prescriptions can be expected to have consequences for the emotional states of the men and women experiencing them.

Historically, the distinctive roles of men and women have been an important mechanism for avoiding otherwise conflicting occupational and family demands. Fathers have been able to concentrate on the breadwinning role and mothers have devoted their attention to childcare (Parsons, 1959; Parsons and Bales, 1966). But conditions have changed, and the employment of wives and mothers may be producing resultant changes in the psychological well-being of parents.

There are two competing views on the psychological effects of maternal employment. One holds that the traditional division of labor between the sexes has been functional and beneficial to both. Consequently, as increasing numbers of mothers perform family and work roles, they should experience an increase in role conflict and its resultant strains. This "role strain" interpretation necessarily assumes that there is a fixed quantity of time, energy, and commitment available for work and family responsibilities (Coser and Rokoff, 1971; Goode, 1960). The hypothesized effects on fathers, from this perspective, are unclear. But given their somewhat greater involvement in childcare, as well as the expectation of involvement (see Pleck, 1985; Juster, 1985; Robinson, 1985; Coverman and Sheley, 1986), one might well assume a correspondingly greater role overload among husbands of employed wives and, consequently, higher levels of mental strain as well.

The second view emphasizes the positive consequences of employment for women's well-being. Research on mental health has consistently revealed higher levels of emotional distress among women than among men (Pearlin and Johnson, 1977; Gove, 1984; Gove and Tudor, 1973; Cleary and Mechanic, 1983; Gore and Mangione, 1983; Bernard, 1972). This gender difference is presumed to arise in part from the more restricted and isolated role played by women in industrialized society (Gove, 1972; Gove and Geerken, 1977; Guttentag et al., 1980). But as women join the labor force, the strains they experience may, as a consequence, be reduced. As Liljeström and colleagues (1978) note in their study of Swedish blue-collar women: "Gainful employment signifies an *opening* for women. *They get out.* It is striking how often they use the phrase 'to get out a bit'" (p. 80). This is consistent with the key assumption of a "multiple identities" hypothesis, which holds that there are benefits to be gained through the accumulation of social identities (Marks, 1977; Sieber, 1974; Thoits, 1986). The evidence is conflicting. Some cross-sectional data have established a positive relationship between employment and the mental health of women in the United States and Canada, but still other studies have found no differences in psychological health between working and nonworking women.[4]

Some have suggested that the development of more egalitarian gender roles can prove beneficial to both men and women, decreasing tensions between husbands and wives and providing for multiple and socially valued roles for both. But these benefits are likely to accrue only to the extent that behavior is congruent with attitudes, that is, when husbands and wives not only share provider and domestic roles but also agree that this is their preferred arrangement (Kessler and McRae, 1984; Ross, Mirowsky, and Huber, 1983).

The life-course approach I follow here incorporates elements from both the role-strain and the identity-enhancement perspectives. Whether maternal employment has deleterious or positive effects depends on the *context* in which it occurs. Thus, the degree to which mothers of young children experience well-being in conjunction with

4. Studies documenting this positive relationship between employment and psychological well-being include Gove and Geerken, 1977; Welch and Booth, 1974; Kessler and McRae, 1982; Gore and Mangione, 1983; Ross, Mirowsky, and Huber, 1983; the finding is confirmed by some longitudinal research (Thoits, 1986).

Studies finding no difference by labor force status include Pearlin, 1975; Radloff, 1975; Cleary and Mechanic, 1983; Shehan, 1984. See also review by Ross and Mirowsky, 1986.

employment is a function of their work and family situations, the resources available to them, and their own, as well as society's, attitudes toward maternal employment (Shehan, 1984; Warr and Parry, 1982). Women who are single parents, who are in the working class, or who have experienced previous strains are all more vulnerable to stress regardless of their employment status (Brown and Harris, 1978; Menaghan and Lieberman, 1986).

Few scholars have considered temporal shifts in the well-being of men, apart from that caused by unemployment. However, some have investigated the impact of wives' employment on husbands' well-being (Kessler and McRae, 1982; Ross, Mirowsky and Huber, 1983). As already noted, greater domestic responsibilities may lead to strains. Alternatively, men who share childcare may experience enhanced self-esteem and well-being (Baruch and Barnett, 1986; Barnett and Baruch, 1987).

But consider the social and cultural context of individual lives, especially shifts in social expectations regarding men's and women's roles. Those who perceive the meshing of work and family roles as personally valuable and culturally sanctioned, who benefit from supportive employment policies and who are encouraged by an ideology of gender equality, should be the least prone to role conflicts and overloads and, consequently, the most likely to benefit from their labor force participation. It follows, therefore, that Swedish parents from 1968 to 1981 should have experienced a reduction in stress, as maternal employment became the rule rather than the exception and, moreover, became popularly and officially sanctioned. The following chapter tests this hypothesis by examining stability and change in the well-being of Swedish parents during this period.

3

The Well-Being of Parents

Women's and men's roles will not really change unless family
institutions also change, but it is not at all clear in what order
and in what direction family life will be transformed. (Giele,
1978, p. 119)

Parents engage in what undoubtedly is the most important activity in any
society: producing and nurturing members of a new generation. Moreover, they do so in the face of various normative and institutional constraints on their lives, such as the conditions of their employment, that
can impair their ability to parent. Parents of young children, as I discussed in Chapter 2, are disproportionately at risk, given the pressures
they typically encounter in building careers while simultaneously establishing their marriages, homes, and families. How well they fare personally also influences their performance as parents. Intuitively, one would
expect parents experiencing psychological problems or frequent fatigue
to be unequal to the job of parenting, to lack the emotional and physical
reserves of energy required to discharge effectively their childcare responsibilities. And the research literature does indeed document more
positive child development outcomes when mothers feel good about
themselves and their employment (Yarrow et al., 1962; Gold and Andres,
1978a,b; Farel, 1980; Hoffman, 1984; Woods, 1972). Piotrkowski (1979)
reports similar findings for fathers.

In this chapter I examine the manner in which Swedish parents have
been affected by the social and institutional changes occurring from the
late 1960s to the early 1980s. Has their well-being measurably improved,
declined, or remained constant during this period? Have fathers fared

better or less well than mothers? Are there significant differences among parents as a function of their location in the occupational structure? And have differences by gender or by social class changed over this time?

I also investigate the well-being of individual men and women as they move through the early years of parenthood, identifying the parents who experience increases in psychological distress and fatigue from one survey to the next, and those who manage to achieve an improved sense of well-being.

Context

Time, process, and context are finally receiving due consideration in sociological perspectives on family and kinship. (Elder,
1984, p. 128)

Most important in establishing a life course perspective is the matter of *context*. Three essential components are gender, socioeconomic status, and historical period.

Gender and Well-Being

A life course perspective suggests that women, more than men, will continue to experience greater strains during the years of childbearing and child-rearing, since women, even in Sweden's postindustrial society, are expected to be both family-centered and achievement-oriented. Men, in contrast, continue to be acknowledged and rewarded much more for their achievements in the labor marketplace than for their performance as parents. Thus, what men and women bring to the years of childbearing and child-rearing—in the form of traditional gender role socialization and expectations—cannot help but influence the structure of their lives and the manner in which they confront emotional challenges. As Liljeström and Dahlström (1981) point out: "Although women and men partake of the same everyday existence they are not conscious of the same things. They have different tasks. They notice different aspects. Put in the same situation they may perceive it from different perspectives. Their aims are separate" (p. 328).

The research literature consistently reports gender differences in psychological distress: women are more likely than men to evidence higher levels of depression and other psychosomatic symptoms. Recall that some scholars explain this gender difference in terms of the limited roles typically open to women in contemporary society (Gove and Tudor, 1973; Gove and Geerken, 1977; Gove, 1972), the dissatisfaction of women with their roles (Ross, Mirowsky, and Ulbrich, 1983; Ross, Mirowsky, and

Huber, 1983), and strains involved in simultaneously managing work and family roles (Aneshensel et al., 1981). There is some evidence that these gender differences in psychological distress are narrowing, possibly in tandem with the convergence of men's and women's roles in society (Kessler and McRae, 1981; Ross, Mirowsky, and Huber, 1983). However, the responsibility women assume for preschool children may well increase their role overloads and moderate the possible beneficial effects of employment. It is plausible, therefore, that even in a society with egalitarian goals gender differences in well-being will persist. Regarding women's lives, Liljeström and colleagues (1978) remark, "Unless their role in the family is changed at the same time, their liberation will be limping and ambiguous" (p. 83).

Socioeconomic Status and Well-Being

A life course perspective also locates parental well-being within the broader sociological context of social stratification. Social class, or social stratification, can be defined as "the hierarchical distribution of power, privilege, and prestige" (Kohn and Schooler, 1983, p. 6). Socioeconomic status is, then, a key indicator of how resources are distributed. Parents in the lower strata invariably have fewer financial, educational, and other resources.

Social scientists in the United States typically portray a continuum of stratification, commonly based on education and social status (see Kohn and Schooler, 1983). Swedish social scientists, on the other hand, categorize individuals into discrete groups or classes based on their relationship to the means of production, their educational qualifications, general social standing, and occupational location (Erikson and Åberg, 1987). Unlike Americans, the majority of whom describe themselves as "middle class," Swedish citizens typically relegate themselves to one of three class levels (upper, middle, working), categories that are closely tied to their political and trade union affiliations. This classification system is commonly used by social scientists in Sweden and also employed by the labor movement, by the political parties, and by government agencies.

Studies have long documented the links between social class and feelings of well-being, but the features of social class responsible for this consistent finding have not been unequivocally established (Hollingshead and Redlich, 1958; Kessler, 1982; Liem and Liem, 1978; Kohn and Schooler, 1983). One might plausibly assume that those in the lower strata have life experiences more productive of stresses and strains, leading to higher overall levels of psychological distress (e.g., Holmes and Rahe, 1967), even under the generally favorable conditions found in the Swedish welfare state. One study which statistically adjusted for the number of adverse life experiences did indeed find that members of the lower class had higher levels of psychological distress than members of other social classes in the face of the same stressful events (Kessler and Cleary, 1980).

Socioecomonic status may also index different conditions of employment. Specific job characteristics, tied to location in the occupational hierarchy, may account, in part at least, for the relationship between psychological well-being and social class. A job's physical and mental demands, as well as the flexibility it affords, may be particularly influential for parental well-being (Miller et al., 1979; Kohn and Schooler, 1983). Those in higher-status jobs are likely to have more freedom, for example, to establish their working hours and coordinate work and family responsibilities.

Parents in different social strata differ in their ability to withstand the economic costs of combining work and family roles. Professionals can more easily afford to purchase family services and labor-saving devices (dining out, household and childcare help, household appliances, etc.) which reduce the demands on their time and energies (Holmstrom, 1973).

Historical Context

Individuals making the transition to parenthood in 1968 are likely to have experienced quite a different social climate than their counterparts in 1981. Social and occupational conditions changed markedly during that thirteen-year period, with the transformation in gender roles quite possibly the greatest change. By the 1980s both parents were increasingly found in the labor force, consistent with Sweden's vigorous promotion of gender equality. The growing congruence between attitudes and behavior concerning men's and women's roles suggests we might expect to find that both sexes experienced less strain in 1981 than in 1968, but the sheer scale and pace of these changes may have created discomfort in those swept up in their path, resulting instead in greater strain. A 1985 report on equality between women and men in Sweden notes that parenthood has undergone distinct changes, "with the result that the maternal and, above all, the paternal role have become unclear and uncertain" (Ministry of Labor, 1985, pp. 49-50).

The central issue I address in this chapter is not so much *whether* parents experience strains, but *under what conditions* these strains are greater or lesser. Clearly life circumstances and the legislative environment changed markedly in the 1970s. But did these developments in fact augur to the benefit of Swedish parents?

The next section places well-being within this context of social change, examining differences in well-being over the thirteen years punctuated by the Level of Living Surveys. The final section charts changes in the reported well-being of two cohorts of individual parents during this period.

Patterns and Trends, 1968–81

Between 1968 and 1981 the early phase of parenthood changed markedly in Sweden, reflecting major changes in Swedish society during this period (see Table 3.1). The notable increase in the work involvement of mothers with pre-schoolers has already been discussed.

While 64 percent of this group were outside the labor force in 1968, by 1981 only 22 percent were not employed. Equally notable though less dramatic changes occurred in the employment experience of Swedish fathers. For example, while nearly four-fifths of them worked more than a 40-hour work week in 1968, less than one in ten did so in 1981. (The full-time work week was reduced from 42.5 hours to 40 hours in 1972.)

Still other changes occurred in tandem with those in labor force involvement. For example, although there appears to have been relative constancy in the distribution of parents among the three socioeconomic classes, the overall educational level of Swedish parents increased markedly. Education has been shown to be positively related to the psychological functioning of both men and women, at least in the United States (Kessler, 1979; Thoits and Hannan, 1979). But the positive implications of this may be offset in Sweden by the increase in the number of single-parent families headed by women, from 4.6 percent in 1968 to 10.3 percent in 1981. Single-parent status has been found to be negatively related to psychological well-being in U.S. studies (Gove, 1972; Pearlin and Johnson, 1977). (In the 1981 sample, fewer than 1 percent of Swedish fathers of preschoolers were raising children on their own.)

Recall too the impressive growth in nonmarital cohabitation. But note that cohabiting couples in Sweden, unlike in the United States, enjoy many of the same legal and social privileges as do married couples, and most see their relationship as on a par with marriage (National Committee, 1979). Indeed, much of the statistical data produced by government agencies typically combine individuals in both statuses: in the Level of Living Survey, respondents are coded as "married or cohabiting." Thus, the increase in single mothers from 4.6 percent in 1968 to 10.3 percent in 1981 represents an increase in the number who were raising children on their own with neither spouse nor companion.

Any number of societal-level historical events, such as a recessionary economy, may have altered the conditions and experiences of parents dur-

Table 3.1. Demographic and other characteristics of parents caring for children[a] in Sweden, 1968, 1974, 1981 (in percentages)

	Fathers			Mothers		
	1968	1974	1981	1968	1974	1981
(N)	(521)	(523)	(446)	(536)	(530)	(501)
Area of residence[b]						
Metropolitan areas	26.6	26.4	27.0	28.4	25.1	27.0
Moderate cities	20.0	19.0	14.3	20.7	23.1	18.5
Small cities	24.1	24.3	22.5	22.2	21.1	22.1
Rural	29.3	30.3	36.1	28.6	30.6	32.4
Marital status						
Married or cohabiting	98.6	99.5	99.2	95.4	92.3	89.7
Single parent	1.4	0.5	0.8	4.6	7.7	10.3
Family size						
1 child only	33.3	35.9	30.9	36.3	35.9	32.2
Education						
Less than gymnasium[c]	93.6	77.3	66.1	90.1	87.1	76.9
Gymnasium degree	4.7	10.2	19.8	4.6	8.9	17.4
University degree	1.7	12.4	14.2	5.3	4.0	5.6
Socioeconomic level[d]						
Upper	11.7	14.0	13.6	7.6	6.9	6.4
Middle	38.2	36.1	39.0	40.5	42.8	45.8
Working	50.1	49.9	47.4	51.9	50.3	47.8
Labor force status						
Not in labor force[e]	3.8	3.8	2.5	63.8	42.7	22.1
In labor force	96.2	96.2	97.5	36.2	57.3	77.9
Work hours (of those employed)[f]						
Less than 20 hr	0.4	0.0	0.6	29.1	19.0	9.3
20-34 hr	1.7	2.3	3.9	31.7	38.7	54.9
35-40 hr	20.0	85.0	86.8	15.9	37.0	32.5
41 hr or more	77.8	12.8	8.8	23.4	5.3	3.2
Percent reporting physical limitations[g]	6.4	3.8	5.7	10.2	7.0	5.6

Source: 1968, 1974, 1981 waves of the Level of Living Survey, Swedish Institute for Social Research, Stockholm University.

[a]Children living at home under 7 years of age.

[b]Large = Stockholm, Göteborg, Malmö; medium = 10,000+; small = 500–10,000; rural = rural area or village of < 500.

[c]Similar to secondary school but more like a junior college degree.

[d]Those in professional occupations depicted as upper class, white-collar service workers as middle class, and manual workers as working class. Women not in the labor force are classified on the basis of previous occupation.

[e]This may include those few who are unemployed at the time of the survey.

[f]Does not include the work hours of the self-employed.

[g]Difficulty in taking a brisk 100-meter walk, running 100 meters, or climbing stairs.

ing the 1968–1981 period. The 1970s were years of turmoil and change in
Sweden, a decade "full of political and economic drama" (Rydén and
Bergström, 1982 p. 1). Constitutional reform, an international economic
crisis, the nuclear power debate, anger and anguish over the Vietnam
War, labor law reform, the end of four decades of Social Democratic control of the government—all these punctuated the years captured in the
Level of Living Surveys (see, for example, Rydén and Bergström, 1982;
Hadenius, 1985). However, there can be no doubt about the importance
of the new social policies of the 1970s (described in Chapter 2) which
aimed to reduce gender inequality and to ease the strains experienced by
working parents. For instance, changes in tax policy, providing for individual rather than family taxation, encouraged the movement of women
of all ages into the labor force. Also, as Sundström (1987) notes, many
social benefits, such as parental leave, provided women with an "insurance motive" for belonging to the labor force. And changes in institutional policies and practices, such as those encouraging part-time
employment and parental leaves of absence, could have had marked
positive effects on employed parents by increasing the degree of freedom
available to them.

   How do we measure the effects, if any, of all these changes on well-
being? To answer this question, data from two measures of well-being are
used: (1) whether parents report experiencing daily fatigue during the
two weeks preceding the survey, and (2) whether they report various
symptoms of psychological distress over the preceding year (see Appendix
A). The absence of tiredness and psychological strain have been shown to
contribute significantly to one's general sense of well-being (Campbell,
1981).

   Recall from Chapter 2 that two alternative theoretical orientations
postulate different effects on parental well-being of changing gender
roles, particularly with regard to the participation of mothers of young
children. The role-strain hypothesis posits increasing strains upon parents, especially mothers, as a result of the cross-pressures of family and
work responsibilities. As Wistrand (1981) notes, being with one's children
is also "work." And for many, "children have become an obstacle, a baby-
sitting problem," while others see their job as the problem, "the job that
deprives them of the opportunity to follow the development of their own
children" (p. 24). The multiple-roles hypothesis suggest that employment
outside the home may improve the emotional health of mothers by
enhancing their personal identities. As two working-class women interviewed in the 1970s said, "when I was at home I had no self-confidence.
It's nice to know that I'm not so stupid as I thought." And, "I've never felt

so good in my life as when I started working. When I was at home I would probe after every single ailment" (Liljeström et al., 1978 p. 79).

If the role-strain hypothesis is correct, one would expect an increase in the proportion of Swedish parents reporting psychological distress during the 1968-1981 survey period. If the multiple-roles hypothesis is valid, then mothers in 1981 should be less likely than their 1968 and 1974 counterparts to report emotional problems, with the effects on fathers unclear.

As can be seen in Figure 3.1, the proportion of Swedish mothers reporting psychological distress appears to have dropped from the late 1960s to the early 1980s. This decline is quite striking, particularly in view of the marked increase in women's labor force participation during this period. These data, then, do provide some preliminary support for the multiple-roles hypothesis.

Does this improvement occur uniformly among different subgroups of women? In Table 3.2, variations in well-being by social class are analyzed with class operationally defined in terms of occupational status (Vuksanovic, 1975; Van Zandt Winn, 1984; Erikson and Åberg, 1987). The upper class consists of professionals (lawyers, architects, doctors, dentists, etc.), administrators, and managers, or what Americans might more comfortably term the "upper middle" class. The middle class is composed of white-collar service workers, small proprietors, and artisans. And manual workers—skilled, semiskilled and unskilled—constitute the working class. Women who are not currently in the labor force are classified on the basis of their last occupations. These groups fairly portray the actual stratification system in Sweden. With few modifications the same classification by position in the system of production has been employed by Swedish investigators for well over a half-century and is still in common use today.

Not surprisingly, there are indeed differences in well-being by socioeconomic level. In the survey, professional–level fathers were more likely than those in the working class to report symptoms of psychological strain (see Table 3.2). This is an unexpected finding, since research has consistently documented a positive relationship between socioeconomic status and psychological functioning. It may reflect the pressures experienced by young professionals in establishing themselves in their careers. However, this does not appear to be the case for women. For mothers, the picture is less clear, but by the 1980s (or even by 1974) it was the working-class mothers who most frequently reported psychological distress; such reports declined in frequency as one moves up the class hierarchy. The prevalence of psychological strain remained stable across the survey years

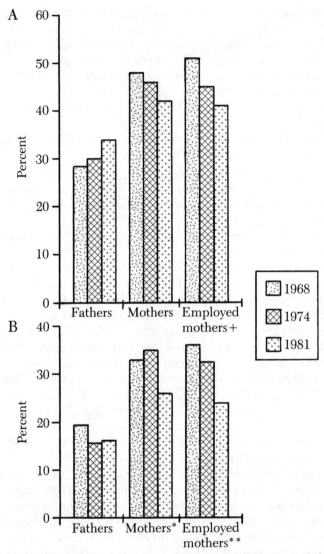

Figure 3.1. The well-being of Swedish parents, 1968–81. A. Daily fatigue in the last two weeks. B. Psychological strain (symptoms of anxiety, depression, etc.) over the last 12 months.

Source: 1968, 1974, 1981 waves of the Level of Living Survey, Swedish Institute for Social Research, Stockholm University.

Differences by year statistically significant at $p < .10$, +; $p < .05$, *; $p < .01$, **.

Table 3.2. Distribution of parental well-being by socioeconomic status[a] and survey year

	Fathers			Mothers		
	1968	1974	1981	1968	1974	1981
(N)	(521)	(523)	(446)	(536)	(530)	(501)
Report symptoms of psychological strain over past 12 months (%)						
Upper	22.6	21.0	21.4	34.8	24.8	16.5
Middle	22.6*	11.9*	12.7*	34.1*	31.5*	24.0*
Working	16.2	17.0	17.2	32.8+	39.8+	30.0+
Average for all levels	19.4	15.7	16.0	33.5*	35.2*	26.4*
Report daily fatigue over past 2 weeks (%)						
Upper	23.7	29.8	24.8	39.4	41.4	43.4
Middle	25.6	26.8	30.8	46.8+	42.6+	36.7+
Working	32.8	32.1	38.3	50.9	50.5	47.2
Average for all levels	29.0	29.9	33.5	48.4	46.5	42.2

Source: 1968, 1974, 1981 waves of the Level of Living Survey, Swedish Institute for Social Research, Stockholm University.

[a]Socioeconomic level is categorized into three groups, with those in professional occupations depicted as upper, white-collar service workers as middle, and manual workers as working. Women not in the labor force are classified on the basis of previous occupation.

*Difference by year significant at $p < .05$.

+Difference by year significant at $p < .10$.

for professional and working class fathers, but not so for those in the middle class, who reported a decline. Middle-class mothers also evidenced a similar decrease in the frequency of psychological distress, while working-class mothers were the most likely to report distress in 1974 and the least likely to do so by 1981.

Turning to the measure of fatigue, it is clear that mothers at every socioeconomic level were more likely to report feeling tired during the previous two weeks than were fathers. But the experience of fatigue by both sexes was differentially distributed by social class; those in the working class typically were the most prone to fatigue.

Stability and Change: Multivariate Models

To determine the factors that primarily account for level of psychological functioning, a multivariate logistic model was applied separately for each criterion of well-being (Selen, 1985). Included in the equation were socioeconomic class (upper, middle, working), area of residence (metropolitan, smaller cities, rural), gender (male, female), age (under 25, 25–34, 35 and older), and survey year (1968, 1974, 1981).

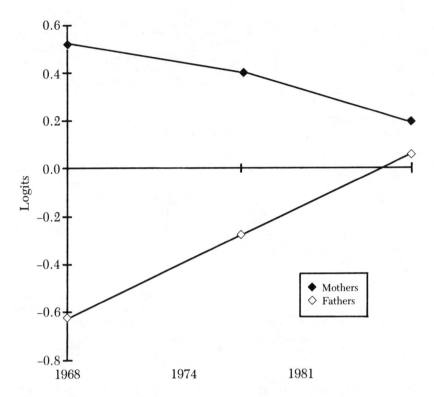

Effect parameters of logit regression model
Model is GYF RYF ASGR
($\chi^2 = 68.17$, d.f. $= 120$, $p = .99$, $N = 3057$)

Figure 3.2. Likelihood of daily fatigue of Swedish parents, by gender and year.
  Source: 1968, 1974, 1981 waves of the Level of Living Survey, Swedish Institute for
Social Research, Stockholm University.
  In logit model, G = gender (male, female); Y = survey year (1968, 1974, 1981);
A = age (under 25, 25–36, 36 and older), R = area of residence (metropolitan, other city,
rural), S = socioeconomic status (upper, middle, working class), F = daily fatigue over
last two weeks (no, yes).

An analysis of the effects of the factors included in the model on the
likelihood of experiencing daily fatigue reveals significant interactions
between survey year and gender (see Figure 3.2). These findings suggest
that, controlling for background factors, fathers had an increased probability (from 1968 to 1981) of reporting feelings of fatigue, whereas the
likelihood that mothers would report fatigue declined slightly during this
period. This is a somewhat surprising finding, insofar as the working
hours of fathers were reduced over this time, while the numbers of mothers in the labor force more than doubled. There seems, then, to be no

simple relationship between the labor force attachment of either parent and feelings of fatigue. Significant changes also occurred over the survey years as a function of residential location: parents living in nonmetropolitan cities were increasingly likely to report feeling tired (Table 3.3).

Turning to the indicator of psychological strain we find, again controlling for background factors, that the most significant predictors of strain across the years of the survey are residential location and an interaction between gender and social class. Parents living in the large metropolitan areas of Sweden were most likely to report psychological symptoms throughout the twelve years of the study.

The interaction between gender and socioeconomic status reveals interesting differences in the distribution of distress for mothers and fathers. As noted earlier, fathers in professional occupations are more likely than those at lower occupational levels to report psychological symptoms. In the case of mothers, however, it is those in the working class who have the greatest probability of experiencing mental strain.

Table 3.3. Multiplicative model[a] estimating parental well-being

The Likelihood of Daily Fatigue			
	Interaction effects[b] by gender and year		
	1968	*1974*	*1981*
Fathers	.728	.869	1.04
Mothers	1.13	1.22	1.10
	Interaction effects by residence and year		
	1968	*1974*	*1981*
Metropolitan areas	1.18	1.07	1.15
Middle and small cities	.802	1.04	1.17
Rural areas	.793	.981	.905

The Likelihood of Reported Mental Strain		
	Interaction effects by gender and socioeconomic level	
	Fathers	*Mothers*
Upper	.917	.754
Middle	.851	1.43
Working	.788	1.52

[a]Logistic regression models include the effects of gender (male, female), survey year (1968, 1974, 1981), age (under 25, 26–35, 36 and older), area of residence (metropolitan, other city, rural), socioeconomic status (upper, middle, working).

[b]The parameter estimates are multiplicative. A parameter greater than 1 indicates a greater than average likelihood of the criterion variable. Less than 1 means a less than average likelihood.

Fit of the model of daily fatigue χ^2 (120) = 68.17

Fit of the model of mental strain χ^2 (120) = 56.26

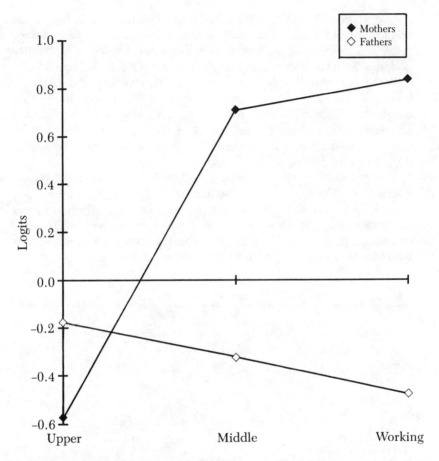

Effect parameters of logit regression model
Model is SGP RP SGYRA
($\chi^2 = 56.26$, d.f. $= 120$, $p = .99$, $N = 3057$)

Figure 3.3. Likelihood of psychological strain of Swedish parents by gender and social class.

Source: 1968, 1974, 1981 waves of the Level of Living Survey, Swedish Institute for Social Research, Stockholm University.

In logit model, G = gender (male, female); Y = survey year (1968, 1974, 1981); A = age (under 25, 25-36, 36 and older), R = area of residence (metropolitan, other city, rural), S = socioeconomic status (upper, middle, working class), P = psychological strain over last 12 months, F = daily fatigue over last two weeks (no, yes).

In general, the likelihood of psychological distress and fatigue became more evenly distributed between parents from 1968 to 1981. Still, more mothers than fathers continued to report both psychological strain and fatigue, in spite of the changes in gender roles.

Stability and Change: Individual Lives

The preceding section used time-series data from the three waves of the Level of Living Survey to document general trends in well-being from 1968 through 1981. This section analyzes the data longitudinally, following individual men and women as they become parents or as their preschoolers move into middle childhood. How did the well-being of individuals change, and what factors account for these changes over time?

The next two chapters will consider the effects of the work environment on well-being. Here I examine the relationships of family and individual characteristics to psychological well-being. Data from two cohorts of parents are analyzed (See Figure 1.1): (1) the 1968–74 cohort consists of those men and women who either had preschool children in 1968 or became parents by 1974; (2) the 1974–81 cohort includes men and women who had preschoolers in 1974 or became parents by 1981. Looking at these two groups can help to disentangle life course effects (i.e., moving from one family stage to another, as in the transition to parenthood) from broader social changes making the conditions of parenting easier or more difficult in 1981 compared to 1968.

Among individual characteristics likely to influence parental well-being are age, education, and location in the class structure; among family characteristics are number of children, marital status, and family life stage. Social class and education should reduce the likelihood of psychological distress and fatigue since parents with higher status and education have greater access to resources with which to cope with their life circumstances (Kessler, 1979; Thoits and Hannan, 1979). Family demands, such as number of children and single parenthood, should increase them. The probable effect of family life stage is more ambiguous. Some researchers maintain that the transition to parenthood is a particularly stressful event (e.g., Rossi, 1968); others argue that it is less psychologically disruptive than often believed (e.g., Pearlin and Lieberman, 1977; Pearlin, 1980).

But the most powerful predictor of current well-being may well be previous well-being. One would expect certain continuities in levels of psychological and physical functioning throughout early adulthood—thus, logically, those who experienced psychological symptoms or fatigue in the past should continue evidencing them. To distinguish the influence of past experience, measures of distress and fatigue in 1968 are included in the analysis of well-being in 1974, and measures taken in 1974 are included in the equations estimating well-being in 1981.

Multivariate regression analysis reveals that, for both men and women in both time periods, levels of distress or fatigue six years earlier are in fact the best predictors of current psychological strain or fatigue (see Table 3.4).

The absence of education effects is surprising. Research on American men and women suggests that educational level has a direct relationship to well-being, even though "educational level" as used here is not strictly analogous to the categories used in United States studies. Possibly the influence of schooling is captured by the measures of previous well-being—that is, less educated respondents may have rated high on strain and fatigue in the previous survey. However, having some university training is not highly correlated with measures of either previous or current well-being.

Becoming a parent or having one's youngest child reach school age seem neither to increase nor decrease, in any direct way, reported symptoms of distress and daily fatigue. But the number of children in the family is relevant for both the 1968–74 and 1974–81 cohorts: having more rather than fewer children reduces the likelihood of psychological distress for Swedish fathers, although not for mothers. Perhaps fathers enjoy the emotional satisfactions children bring without tending—and attending—to their daily demands as closely as do mothers.

Social class affects both psychological distress and fatigue in the 1974–81 cohort, but these effects vary by gender and by symptom. As with the time-series data, fathers in professional jobs and working-class mothers are more likely to report increased symptoms of psychological strain. By contrast, working-class fathers are likely to report an increase in fatigue, whereas working-class mothers are less likely to report fatigue in 1981.

Finally, it is not surprising that physical health limitations are typically related to increases in both fatigue and psychological distress.

Why are men who are managers or professionals more prone to psychological distress than those lower in the occupational hierarchy? They certainly possess more rewards and resources—power, privilege, prestige—that should promote well-being. But the male professionals I interviewed appeared caught up in their work. The most stressful aspects of their jobs seemed also to be conditions that were absorbing of psychic energy, such as "internal organizational matters," "ambitions for self and for department," "being the ultimate decision-maker."

Table 3.4. Likelihood of psychological strain and daily fatigue for Swedish parents of young children, 1974 and 1981 (Metric coefficients)

	Fathers				Mothers			
	Psychological strain[a]		Daily fatigue[b]		Psychological strain		Daily fatigue	
	1974	1981	1974	1981	1974	1981	1974	1981
(N)	(678)	(676)	(678)	(676)	(785)	(721)	(785)	(721)
Individual characteristics								
Age	−.003	.056	.088+	.004	−.041	.009	−.162**	−.022
Education[c]	−.045	−.060	.029	−.050	.005	.034	.071	−.060
Physical limitations[d]	.076*	.084*	−.009	.164***	.103**	.102**	.092**	.115**
Socioeconomic level[e]								
Upper	.080	.121*	−.042	.072	.046	−.026	−.010	.006
Working	.020	.060	−.021	.886*	.091*	.085*	.085*	−.135
Residence[f]								
Metropolitan	.035	−.041	.082*	.057	.001	−.041	.024	.081*
Rural	.020	.013	.064	−.018	−.013	−.029	−.003	.001
Previous strain[g]	.750***	.272***	.140***	.210***	.222***	.308***	.155***	.165***
Previous fatigue[g]	.200***	.079*	.179***	.128***	.104***	.087*	.113**	.089*
Family characteristics								
Number of children	−.120**	−.082*	−.035	−.008	−.056	−.058	.003	.034
Family stage[h]								
New parents	−.064	−.066	−.025	−.014	−.049	−.003	.057	−.021
Middle childhood	.017	−.043	−.003	−.020	−.025	.055	−.052	−.004
R^2 (adjusted)	.056	.115	.034	.117	.091	.136	.074	.058

Source: 1968, 1974, 1981 waves of the Level of Living Survey, Swedish Institute for Social Research, Stockholm University.

Note: Two cohorts of parents are examined, looking at changes in psychological strain or daily fatigue between 1968–74 and 1974–81. Respondents are included in the first sample (1968–74) if they either had a preschooler in 1968 or became parents by 1974. Similarly, respondents in the 1974–81 cohort either had a preschooler in 1974 or became parents by 1981.

[a] Reported symptoms of psychological distress over past year.

[b] Reported symptoms of daily fatigue over past two weeks.

[c] Education beyond gymnasium degree (similar to junior college degree).

[d] Difficulty in taking a brisk 100-meter walk, running 100 meters, or climbing stairs.

[e] Middle class omitted category.

[f] Middle-sized cities omitted category.

[g] Reported symptoms of psychological distress or fatigue previous survey year (i.e. 1968 for 1968–74 cohort, and 1974 for 1974–81 cohort).

[h] Having preschoolers present both years omitted category.

+$p < .10$; *$p < .05$; **$p < .01$; ***$p < .001$.

Interaction Effects

Family stage apparently has no straightforward effect on the emotional health of parents. However, this finding (documented in the coefficients reported in Table 3.4) represents linear effects, that is, the direct effect of each variable on the likelihood of strain or fatigue. Equally interesting are possible *interaction* effects, the combined or contingent influence of two or more variables on well-being. Figure 3.4 presents an example of such an interaction, that between family stage and previous emotional health for fathers. Fathers who reported psychological strain in 1974 and whose children moved into middle childhood are also the most likely to report strain in 1981. This contingency is equally true for men just

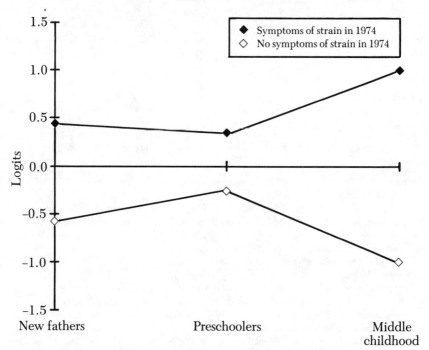

Effect parameters (lambdas) of logit model controlling for work demands
Model is PSO PD SDAWO (G^2 = 51.85, d.f. = 55, p = .59, N = 644)

Figure 3.4. Likelihood of psychological strain of Swedish fathers, 1981, by life stage and previous strain.

Source: 1974, 1981 waves of the Level of Living Survey, Swedish Institute for Social Research, Stockholm University.

New fathers = fathers with preschoolers in 1981 but not in 1974; Preschoolers = fathers with preschoolers in both 1974 and 1981; Middle childhood = fathers with pre-schoolers in 1974 and school-aged children in 1981. A = workplace autonomy, D = job demands, O = previous strains (no, yes), P = psychological strains (no, yes), S = family stage (new fathers, preschoolers both years, middle childhood), W = wife employed (no, yes).

becoming fathers; the transition is more stressful for those who have previously experienced psychological strains.[1] The increased propensity for
psychological distress among fathers "at risk" as their children reach
school age could reflect growing job pressures, as they (and their children) grow older. As the Swedish report on gender equality remarked,
"The identity of many men is completely bound up with their occupational role. They do not have many contacts outside their work. They put
their souls into their jobs and are often intensely preoccupied with their
responsibilities for supporting the family" (Ministry of Labor, 1985,
p. 82).

Variations by family stage are also found for women in both the
1968–74 and 1974–81 cohorts. Those who became mothers within the
previous seven years were the most likely to report distress, and those in
the working class were slightly more prone to psychological distress (see
Figure 3.5). The higher likelihood of distress for women who more
recently made the transition to motherhood is not surprising, given the
radical shifts in identity, life style, and responsibilities entailed in becoming a mother. These life stage findings are exclusive of other factors influencing distress in women, including marital status (less strain for
married), year (less strain in 1981 than in 1974), and previous level of
strain (those evincing high levels of strain in the previous survey were
most prone to strain in the current survey).

Family stage also interacts with women's marital status in predicting
fatigue. Unmarried (and noncohabiting) mothers were the most likely to
report fatigue, especially as their children moved into the middle years of
childhood (see Figure 3.6). Again, those most likely to report fatigue in
1981 were, not surprisingly, mothers who reported fatigue in the 1974
survey.

Models depicting interactions in estimating the daily fatigue of fathers
are more complex and will be discussed in Chapter 5.

Quality of Life

A frequently employed measure of well-being is a rating of one's general
life situation (see Campbell et al., 1976; Campbell, 1981). The 1981 wave
of the Level of Living Survey asked respondents to rank their conditions
of life on a five-point scale ranging from "very good" to "very bad"; most
rated their life situations as either "very good" or "quite good." Variation
in the perceived quality of life was related to a number of family

---

1. Nearly 40 percent of the fathers whose preschoolers moved into the middle years of
childhood were over thirty-five, compared to about 9 percent of new fathers, of whom 80
percent were under thirty years of age.

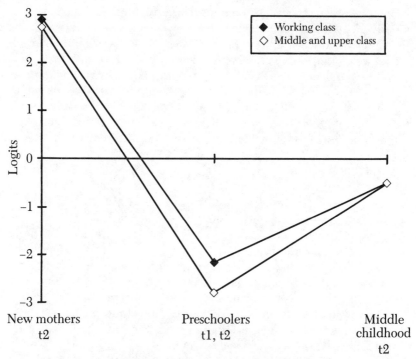

Effect parameters (lambdas) of logit model controlling for marital status, previous strains, and year (1974, 1981)
Model is OP MP PT CSP OMSCT (G^2 = 160, d.f. = 142, p = .142, N = 1506)
Figure 3.5. Likelihood of psychological strain of Swedish mothers, 1974 and 1981, by social class and family life stage.
    Source: 1968, 1974, 1981 waves of the Level of Living Survey, Swedish Institute for Social Research, Stockholm University.
    New mothers = mothers with preschoolers in years indicated; Preschoolers = mothers with preschoolers in years indicated; Middle childhood = mothers with preschoolers and school-aged children, respectively, for years indicated. t1 = 1968 for the 1968–74 cohort, 1974 for the 1974–81 cohort; t2 = 1974 for the 1968–74 cohort, 1981 for the 1974–81 cohort. C = social class (upper and middle, working), M = marital status (married/cohabiting, not married/cohabiting), O = previous strains (no, yes), P = psychological strain (no, yes), S = family stage (new fathers, preschoolers both years, middle child-hood), W = employment (working, not working), T = time (1968–74 cohort, 1974–81 cohort).

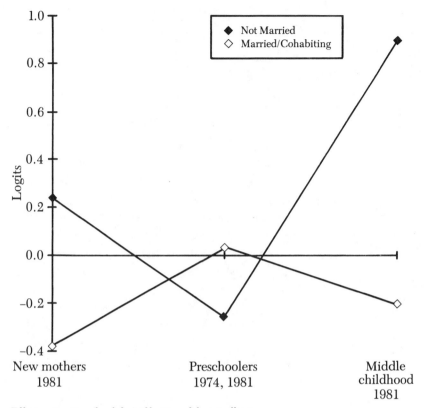

Effect parameters (lambdas) of logit model controlling
for previous (1974) fatigue
Model is FMS XF WXMCS ($G^2 = 95.63$, d.f. $= 70$, $p = .023$, $N = 721$)

Figure 3.6. Likelihood of daily fatigue of Swedish mothers, 1981, by marital status and family life stage.

Source: 1974, 1981 waves of the Level of Living Survey, Swedish Institute for Social Research, Stockholm University.

New mothers = mothers with preschoolers in 1981 but not in 1974; Preschoolers = mothers with preschoolers in both 1974 and 1981; Middle childhood = mothers with preschoolers in 1974 and school-aged children in 1981. C = social class (upper and middle, working), F = daily fatigue (no, yes), M = marital status (married/cohabiting, not married/cohabiting), S = family stage (new fathers, preschoolers both years, middle childhood), W = employment (working, not working), X = previous fatigue (no, yes).

Table 3.5. Assessment of life conditions of Swedish parents, 1974–81 cohort (metric coefficients)

	Mothers	Fathers
(N)	(675)	(720)
Individual characteristics		
Age	1.100*	.085+
Education[a]	-.131*	-.055
Physical limitations[b]	.117**	-.009
Socioeconomic level[c]		
Upper	-.061	-.068+
Lower	.104*	.150***
Residence[d]		
Metropolitan	-.008	-.054
Rural	-.032	-.012
Previous strain[e]	.114	.122**
Previous fatigue[e]	.038	.025
Family characteristics		
Number of children	-.068+	-.100*
Family stage[f]		
New parents	-.045	-.031
Middle childhood	-.079	-.016
R^2 (adjusted)	.09	.06

Source: 1974, 1981 waves of the Level of Living Survey, Swedish Institute for Social Research, Stockholm University.

Note: A positive coefficient means a more negative assessment of life conditions.

[a]Education beyond gymnasium degree (similar to junior college degree).

[b]Difficulty in taking a brisk 100-meter walk, running 100 meters, or climbing stairs.

[c]Middle class omitted category.

[d]Middle-sized cities omitted category.

[e]Reported symptoms of psychological distress previous survey year (i.e., 1968 for 1968–74 cohort, and 1974 for 1974–81 cohort).

[f]Having preschoolers present both years omitted category.

$+p < .10; *p < .05; **p < .01; ***p < .001.$

and individual characteristics (see Table 3.5). For example, working-class parents were less positive in their evaluations than those in the higher strata, and older parents were less positive than younger ones. But for women as well as men, the more children the higher the rating. And, for fathers, having some university education also improved the rating.

Conclusions

What do the Level of Living survey data reveal about the well-being of parents in Swedish society? First is an apparent narrowing in the gap between the well-being of men and women.

The reported psychological distress of mothers declined from 1968 to

1981, and their reported daily physical fatigue remained fairly stable, even declining slightly by 1981. In contrast, the reported daily fatigue of fathers, controlling for background variables, increased over this period. It is clear that the emotional and energy levels of parents are different in 1981 than they were in 1968, concurrently with the influx of mothers into the labor force and the significant policy changes that altered the context and conditions of parenting. The well-being of men and women appears, indeed, to be converging—a trend that has also been observed in the United States (Kessler and McRae, 1981; Ross, Mirowsky, and Huber, 1983). Still, mothers of young children continue to be more likely than fathers to report fatigue or psychological distress across all years of this survey.

Second, social class, like gender, is vitally important in predicting well-being. Working-class mothers are the most prone to experience psychological distress, whereas fathers in professional occupations are most vulnerable to such strain. These differences by socioeconomic status remain stable throughout the three time periods under study. Parents in the working class are also more likely to report physical fatigue and to be less positive in assessing the quality of their lives. These findings testify to the enduring and pervasive influence of social class even in a society dedicated to removing or at least reducing the inequalities associated with position in the class structure.

Third, the resources that individuals bring to the parenting years, in the form of energy level and freedom from psychological strain, have an important influence on subsequent well-being. Those reporting fatigue or distress in one survey were also apt to report it six or seven years later, in the next survey. In fact, the most powerful predictor of present symptoms of distress or fatigue is the past measures of these states. Thus, it would appear that in a postindustrial society, as in previous eras, those who manage best are those who have a history of doing so.

Also important, in combination with other factors, is stage in the life cycle. Specifically, in 1981 fathers of children moving into grade-school years were more likely than fathers of infants and preschoolers to report symptoms of psychological distress, but only if they had previously reported such symptoms in the 1974 survey. By contrast, women who became mothers between surveys were more prone to distress than those with older preschool or school-age children. And being a single parent increased the likelihood of women's strain, regardless of their stage in the life cycle (there were too few single fathers for separate analysis).

Most likely to report daily fatigue were single-parent mothers of school-aged children, despite the greater social resources available to Swedish than to American women in this position. Thus, having a spouse or cohabitant appears to be important in mitigating both emotional strain and physical fatigue.

Why are Swedish mothers better off psychologically in 1981 than in 1974 and 1968? Why are fewer working mothers reporting fatigue at the same time that growing numbers of fathers are doing so? Social policies adopted during this period may have given mothers more options and, hence, greater flexibility in allocating time between workplace and home. And, as I speculated earlier, maternal employment itself may provide women with an additional, psychologically enhancing role identity, while their employment simultaneously invokes more family demands on husbands and fathers. Sandqvist (1987), in her study of Swedish fathers of preschoolers, found that younger fathers had both a lower appraisal of themselves as well as a greater involvement in childcare. Fathers, she suggests, are experiencing rising personal expectations regarding their family role. Indeed, shifts in gender roles may have increased the ambiguity and hence the strain surrounding fatherhood. As reporter Gunder Anderson (1986) remarks: "The Swedish man is the world champion at equality between the sexes. This has made him confused about where to draw the line and how to play the game" (p. 13). Many women, in contrast, are seeing their opportunities expand. A twenty-six-year-old mother and kindergarten teacher explains, "Swedish girls are confident they can manage by themselves—they have jobs—they are helped by the Government" (Burnley, 1985, p. 26). The following chapters examine possible explanations of gender differences as well as the apparent convergence in well-being.

4

Working Conditions of Parents

As the paid work role has evolved in modern society, it has come to call for full time, continuous work from the end of one's education to retirement, desire to actualize one's potential to the fullest, and subordination of other roles to work. This conception of the work role has been, in effect, the male model of the work role. (Pleck, 1977, p. 245)

This chapter examines changes in the working conditions of Swedish parents during the 1970s, addressing the following questions: What are their typical working hours and other employment conditions? How does the work environment of mothers compare to that of fathers? In what ways does the nature of work life vary by location in the occupational structure? And, most important, did the employment conditions of parents change markedly after the late 1960s, as a consequence of various legislative reforms adopted in the 1970s?

The aim here is to set the stage for subsequent analyses of the relationships between specific conditions of work and individual well-being. But before examining the distribution of and changes in various occupational characteristics, I take a more detailed look at the revolutionary change in women's labor force participation.

Life Course Transitions and Maternal Employment

Until recently . . . sociology tended to segregate women off into the institution of the family, as did the rest of society. Women were all but forgotten in mainstream sociology—especially as active participants in occupational and organizational life. (Sokoloff, 1980, p. 1)

For parents of preschool children the most significant employment development has been the growth in the numbers of mothers, especially of preschoolers entering and remaining in the labor force: nearly 80 percent in Sweden in 1981, compared to less than 40 percent in 1968. Tracing the individual behavior of women in two cohorts (1968–74 and 1974–81) permits an analysis of how changes in parenting obligations affected employment behavior at two contiguous but relatively distinct periods: the early and the late 1970s.

In the 1968–74 cohort (see Figure 4.1) we find that women who had preschool children in the home both in 1968 and 1974 were the most likely to remain out of the labor force in each of these years; over a third of this group was not employed at either time. The group most likely to be employed in both 1968 and 1974 consisted of childless women who became mothers by 1974; fully two-fifths of these new mothers had a stable attachment to the labor force. The stronger attachment of recent mothers may reflect the benefit to working mothers, even in the early 1970s, of the paid leave of absence. Since these benefits were considerably enhanced in and after 1974, it could be expected that by 1981 mothers of preschoolers would be even more likely to remain in the labor force, as would pregnant women (see also Sundström, 1987).

Tracking women who became mothers by 1981 reveals that only 6 percent were not employed either before or after the birth of their child. Less than 20 percent of the mothers who had preschoolers in the home both in 1974 and 1981 remained out of the labor force in each of those years, and only 13 percent of the mothers whose preschoolers reached school age stayed out of the labor force. By the early 1980s Swedish women were no longer leaving the labor force because of changes in their family responsibilities. In fact, as we shall see below, it appears that moving into part-time work or taking advantage of the paid leave option have become the preferred means of combining work and family obligations, rather than remaining out of or leaving the labor force.

The United States presents a far different picture. Although strictly comparable data for all mothers of young children are not available, in 1968 the labor force participation rate of married women with preschool children was 27.6 percent; the percentage moved up to 34.4 in 1974, 48.9 in 1981 (Women's Bureau, 1983), and 54 in 1986 (compared to the Swedish rate of 86 percent). Thus, although the proportion of American mothers in the labor force has significantly increased over time, it has not begun to approach the high rates found in Sweden.

The progressive movement of women with young children into employment is, of course, a trend in all industrialized countries, but Sweden is in the forefront of this movement. Erikson (1987) suggests that the

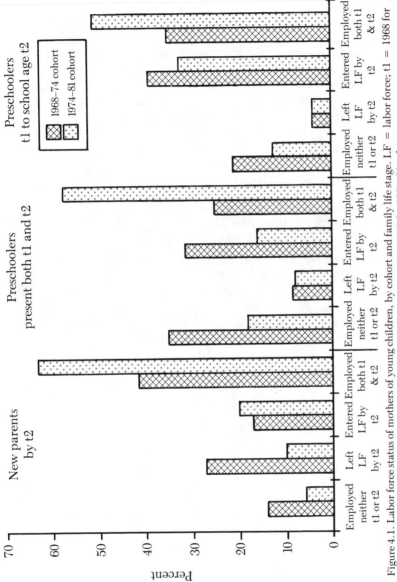

Figure 4.1. Labor force status of mothers of young children, by cohort and family life stage. LF = labor force; t1 = 1968 for 1968–74 cohort, 1974 for 1974–81 cohort; t2 = 1974 for 1968–74 cohort, 1981 for 1974–81 cohort.

Source: 1968, 1974, 1981 waves of the Level of Living Survey, Swedish Institute for Social Research, Stockholm University.

classification of "housewife" may soon disappear in Sweden, as women who now fit this label move either into employment or the retirement years and other, younger women form stable attachments to the labor force.

What is not clear are the working conditions under which mothers are employed, or, for that matter, the workplace conditions of fathers of young children. Parents in advanced societies are said to be moving toward a more symmetrical division of labor (Young and Willmott, 1973; Giele, 1978; Pleck, 1985), in that both mothers and fathers hold jobs during the time they raise their children. But do they work under similar employment conditions?

Working Hours, Schedules, and Leaves of Absence

Most of the daylight hours, most days of the week and year, the
children are one place and their parents are somewhere else.
(Bohen and Viveros-Long, 1981, p. 3)

Possibly no working condition is more central to family life than the time and timing of working hours. Given the physical separation of work and home, time on the job is inevitably time spent away from the family. Moreover, time at work can also interfere with family life by producing parental fatigue and making parents unavailable for family activities. Raising and caring for children undeniably takes a great deal of time, but working parents must also devote a substantial portion of their waking hours to their jobs. Thus today's parents, more than ever before, must reconcile potentially conflicting family and employment responsibilities, and time has become a particularly scarce resource. (See Bohen and Viveros-Long, 1981; Kanter, 1977; Kingston and Nock, 1985; Nock and Kingston, 1984, 1988.)

A number of Swedish parents I interviewed in 1983 and 1985 described time as the most stress-producing feature of their jobs. A professional writer, the mother of a thirteen-month-old boy, said, "I have no way to pace myself because the demands of my child and home are fixed and high." A company department head, the father of two children aged six and sixteen, acknowledged the stress he experienced in trying to fulfill his own and his department's ambitions "without working all the time."

How can such parents simultaneously manage both roles? One obvious way of reducing time pressures is simply to limit the hours spent on the job. But the manner in which time is apportioned between work and family activities varies significantly by gender. In fact, *nothing* distinguishes the employment experiences of Swedish mothers and fathers more than the amount of time each group spends working.

Part-Time

This gender difference is especially evident in the prevalence of part-time employment. Fully two-thirds of Swedish mothers of preschoolers worked less than 35 hours a week in 1981, compared to only 4 percent of fathers. Part-time employment is a particularly important means of resolving the dilemma faced by single parents: nearly four-fifths of the single-parent mothers in the labor force worked only part time.

The popularity of part-time work among Swedish women with families is not a new development. Nearly the same proportions of employed mothers were working part time in 1968 and 1974 as in 1981. What did change from the late 1960s was the *number* of hours constituting part-time work. Whereas in 1968 nearly half of the part-timers worked fewer than 20 hours a week, by 1981 less than 15 percent of the part-timers were on such short hours. The distribution of part-time employment across occupational groups also changed. In 1968 there was a statistically significant relationship between the incidence of part-time hours and occupational level, with working-class women the most likely to be working fewer than 35 hours a week. By 1981, however, the incidence of part-time hours was more equally distributed across all occupational groups (see Table 4.1).

Although part-time employment is a popular choice of Swedish mothers, it does entail certain trade-offs. A mother of two preschoolers who worked six hours a day told me that one of the most stressful aspects of her employment was "not being able to finish a job because of coming home in the afternoon." Others I interviewed also voiced concern about receiving slower promotions and being able to advance to supervisory positions.

Overtime

The obverse of part-time employment is overtime, and here too men's experience differs significantly from that of women's. In 1981 10 percent of Swedish fathers of preschoolers worked more than 40 hours a week, compared to only 3 percent of employed mothers. Still more striking is the sizable reduction in hours of work from the late 1960s to the early 1980s: in 1968 more than three-fourths of fathers had worked over 40 hours a week, but in 1972 Sweden redefined "full-time" from 42.5 to 40 hours per week.

Despite these changes, the long arm of the job is still prominent in the daily lives of many Swedish parents. One professional couple I interviewed—both company executives and the parents of three children, the youngest three years of age—reported that their working hours take a tremendous toll on family life. Even though they employ an *au pair* girl

Table 4.1. Changes in the incidence of part-time employment, leaves of absence, and work flexibility of employed Swedish parents[a] by occupational levels

	Fathers (%)			Mothers (%)		
	1968	1974	1981	1968	1974	1981
(N)	(521)	(523)	(446)	(204)	(305)	(390)
Working part time (< 35 hr)						
Upper[b]	9.2	16.2	4.3	33.6	65.0	52.7
Middle	3.9	4.4	6.7	50.8*	59.6*	70.1*
Working	0.4*	0.4*	6.8*	72.6	48.1	65.3
Average for all levels	2.6*	3.9*	6.4*	62.2	59.1	66.8
On leave of absence last year						
Upper[b]	8.8	11.7	13.7	20.3	30.6	28.2
Middle	4.6	3.3	4.4	26.6	27.2	36.0
Working	2.7	5.2	5.3	6.1*	19.1*	23.3*
Average for all levels	4.1	5.4	6.1	16.2*	23.6*	30.3*
Able to leave job for 30 min without reporting to superior						
Upper[b]	58.8	60.8	68.1	41.9	43.8	53.1
Middle	60.2	65.7	67.5	17.7	24.2	31.0
Working	35.1*	40.0*	50.1*	26.3	27.5	29.4
Average for all levels	46.2*	50.8*	58.4*	23.2	27.1	31.9

Source: 1968, 1974, 1981 waves of the Level of Living Survey, Swedish Institute for Social Research, Stockholm University.

*Statistically significant differences by survey year, $p < .05$.

[a]Parents with children under age 7.

[b]Occupational level is categorized into three groups, with those in professional occupations depicted as upper, white-collar service workers as middle, and manual workers as working. Women not in the labor force are classified on the basis of their previous occupation.

and use a day care center, the husband cites "long working days, much travelling demands, extra backup at home" and "cannot fully control my time" as factors contributing to work-family conflicts. His wife agrees that "work takes both time and emotional resources away from family life with small children." And a teacher, married to a farmer and the mother of three, reports that full-time teaching combined with part-time farm work results in "working hours ranging between 6 am and 8 pm."

Desired Working Hours

The actual working hours of employed parents do not, of course, necessarily correspond to their work-time preferences. Working hours—at leasts in the United States—are typically imposed by employers rather than fashioned by employees. Are Swedish parents satisfied with the amount of time they spend on their jobs? Has their level of satisfaction changed over the years as more opportunities for part-time employment have become available? And how do their preferences and satisfactions vary by gender and by occupational level?

Since questions regarding preferred hours were asked only in the 1974 and 1981 Level of Living Surveys, we have no information as to how parents felt about their hours on the job in 1968. However, the 1974 and 1981 data reveal little change during this period; most parents in both years expressed satisfaction with their present hours (see Table 4.2). There is, however, a gender difference: about 20 percent of the employed mothers but only 12 percent of the fathers wished to work fewer hours in 1981. Mothers with part-time jobs in 1981 were more likely to express satisfaction with their hours than those working 35 hours or more a week. Fully half of this latter group, those working full time and overtime, said that they would prefer to spend less time on the job. Among fathers, those who would most prefer fewer hours work more than 40 hours a week; one-fifth of these "overtimers" wished they could work less. Impressive, too, is the finding that those preferring fewer hours would be willing to accept a corresponding reduction in wages.

Several of the parents I interviewed also said they would prefer fewer hours on the job. One first-time mother, currently on leave to care for her eight-month-old daughter, planned to change to a half-time schedule in her job as an associate magazine editor, saying "the first or early years of my child are so few and I enjoy them, feeling privileged being able to

Table 4.2. Work-hour preferences of employed Swedish parents

	Fathers (%)		Mothers (%)	
	1974	1981	1974	1981
(N)	(523)	(446)	(305)	(390)
Preferring no change	84.0	84.3	74.5	76.2
Fewer hours	12.6	12.1	21.7	19.7
More hours	3.3	3.6	3.8	4.0
Total[a]	99.9	100	100	99.9
Preferring fewer hours, by present work hours				
Long part-time (20–34 hr)	—	—	0.9	4.4
Full time	11.8	11.7	50.7	47.8
Overtime	26.3	12.9	45.0	55.2

Source: 1968, 1974, 1981 waves of the Level of Living Survey, Swedish Institute for Social Research, Stockholm University.

[a]Totals may not equal 100% because of rounding. — indicates insufficient data to report.

share them with her by reducing my working time." Another mother, a nurse's assistant with two preschoolers who was married to a construction worker, would like to reduce her 75 percent time to half time "to be with the children more if we could afford it."

Only 4 percent of the parents in the 1981 survey reported that they would prefer to work more hours. Among mothers, these were principally women working fewer than 20 hours a week; one in ten of these women desired more hours on the job. The fathers preferring more hours were typically those who were employed part time, a fact that suggests that for them part-time work was often not a voluntary choice.

Scheduling

As important as the number of working hours is their timing, particularly for that considerable portion of the labor force employed during nontraditional hours of the day or night (see also Staines and Pleck, 1983; Pleck and Staines, 1985; Presser and Cain, 1983). As Kanter points out, "family events and routines are built around work rhythms (at least more generally than the reverse), just as much of the timing of events in the society as a whole . . . is predicated on assumptions about the hours, days, and months when people are most likely to be working or not working" (1977, p. 31).

Also of concern is the synchronization of schedule among family members. Illustrating the problem is a district manager I interviewed in Stockholm, the father of two and the husband of a dental assistant. He reported that his work and family roles most conflicted "when I and my family can't get our times to mix."

One way for parents to mesh work schedules in order to provide for childcare is to have one work on a job that requires or permits shift work. But this arrangement may not solve the problem if the "free" hours of one parent do not correlate with those of the other or with the time required for childcare. Rotating shifts have been shown to be the most problematic for reconciling work and parenting roles in the United States, whereas night shifts often produce strains in marital relations (Staines and Pleck, 1983; Mott, 1965; Kingston and Nock, 1985; Nock and Kingston, 1984).

Fully a fifth of the Swedish parents studied worked between the hours of 6 P.M. and 10 P.M. in 1981, only slightly fewer than did so in 1968. Moreover, a sixth of the employed parents reported in 1981 that they did some work on weekends, down from more than a fourth in 1968.

Although about equal proportions (four-fifths) of employed mothers and fathers in Sweden worked regular day schedules, more mothers than fathers of young children worked on evening shifts (9 percent compared to 3 percent) and fathers were more likely to be on some other schedule (8

percent compared to 4 percent of employed mothers). About eq
portions (6-7 percent) of mothers and fathers reported working ii
or varying schedules in 1981. Women working part-time hours were far
less likely than full-time workers to have normal daytime schedules.
There were also differences in the prevalence of shift work by occupational level. Parents in working-class jobs were the most likely either to be
engaged in shift work or to work irregular hours.

Leaves of Absence

Gender differences in work-time in Sweden are also revealed in the extent
to which individuals take parental leaves of absence. In 1981, 32 percent
of the employed mothers of preschoolers in our sample reported that they
had been on leave at some time in the previous year, compared to only 6
percent of the fathers. There are class differences as well in the use of this
leave benefit: nearly 14 percent of the men in professional occupations
took a leave, compared to 5 percent of fathers in middle- and working-
class jobs (see Table 4.1). By contrast, it is the mothers in middle-class
jobs who are most likely to use leaves of absence. Nearly two-fifths of
them were on leave at some time in 1980, compared to about a fourth of
those in professional and working-class jobs.

Over these years the numbers of mothers of preschoolers taking leaves
steadily increased. In 1968, 16 percent had been on leave in the previous
year; the number had risen to 24 percent by 1974 and to 32 percent by
1981. The most significant change in leave-taking occurred among
women in working-class jobs—from 6 percent in 1967 to 23 percent in
1980 (see Table 4.1).

Data on current leaves of absence (that is, the week preceding the survey) are available only for 1974 and 1981. Here again, differences by
gender appear: in 1981, 22 percent of the employed mothers were on
leave the previous week, compared to less than 2 percent of the fathers.
The widespread availability and utilization of the parental leave benefit
make labor force participation rates somewhat misleading; to be sure, 86
percent of the mothers of preschoolers were in the labor force in 1986, but
only 56 percent were actually at work (Sundström, 1987).

In 1983 and 1985 I interviewed fathers who then were on or had taken
parental leaves of absence; typically, they expressed surprise at the
amount of time and effort required to care for an infant. One first-time
father (a social scientist in nonacademic employment) had planned to use
the leave to write a book. Instead, he found himself "falling into bed exhausted at the end of the day" after being fully preoccupied by his infant
daughter. Other fathers who had not taken leaves discussed the subtle
and not so subtle pressures from bosses and coworkers to remain on the

job in order to meet deadlines or goals. A report by a subcommittee of the Ministry of Labor (1986) on the changing male role notes, in this regard, that "men who are willing to take paid leave of absence for care of their children frequently encounter the derision and ridicule of their colleagues at work, particularly if the workplace is predominately male" (p. 20).

A U.S. Comparison

The gender differences in working hours and schedules among Swedish parents are, in some respects, not far different from those characterizing parents in the United States. Like their Swedish counterparts, American fathers are more likely to put in longer hours and to start earlier and end later in the day than their wives (Pleck and Staines, 1985; Staines and Pleck, 1983; Moen and Dempster-McClain, 1987).

As in Sweden too, part-time employment is an option elected by many American mothers of young children. It is an especially popular choice for women who hold strong career as well as strong family values, offering to many a means of optimally balancing their two roles (Favor, 1984; Moen and Smith, 1986). Although few mothers of preschoolers in the United States work continuously in part-time jobs, over 40 percent combine periods of part-time work with periods of full-time employment and intervals out of the labor force while their children are at home, and many continue to do so once their children have begun school (Moen, 1985). But although many American women work part time at some point in their lives, part-time work is not nearly so prevalent at any stage of the life course in the United States as it is in Sweden. American men, like Swedish men, are less likely than women to work part-time schedules; those who do so typically work fewer hours involuntarily, in response to slack labor demand (Women's Bureau, 1983).

Recognize also, as earlier noted, that part-time employment has different meanings in the United States and in Sweden. Swedish mothers who work part time are often taking advantage of a legislated benefit which allows them to shorten their working hours while their children are preschoolers. They retain their fringe benefits and can increase their working hours, as they wish, once their children move into school age. In the United States, temporary reductions of working hours are typically difficult to obtain and often require accepting jobs that pay less and have no fringe benefits or job security. Thus the actual number of parents who work part time in the United States does not represent the number who might wish to work a reduced schedule. Data from a 1977 national survey of employed persons in the United States (the Quality of Employment Survey—see Quinn and Staines, 1979) reveal that over half the mothers of children under age twelve in two-earner families and nearly two-fifths of the fathers would prefer to work fewer hours in order to spend more time with their families. Moreover, employed mothers in part-time jobs are the most satisfied with their current hours (Moen and Dempster-McClain, 1987).

Roughly equal numbers of American men and women work schedules other than regular daytime shifts. In about one-third (32.9 percent) of families, one or both spouses start work at other than regular daytime hours (Staines and Pleck, 1983; Presser and Cain, 1983). This arrangement is particularly common among parents with preschoolers, who often use different shifts as a way of sharing childcare responsibilities, and is most true of working-class parents, who elect shift work in order to take turns with "shifts" of childcare (Lein et al., 1974).

American fathers tend to be heavily engaged in some degree of overtime work. Fully 70 percent of fathers of preschoolers generally worked more than 40 hours a week in 1976 (Moen and Moorehouse, 1983). The decline in the working hours of Swedish men in the 1970s has had no parallel in the United States, where American fathers continue to put in comparatively long hours on the job.

There are no reliable national data on parental leaves of absence in the United States. Suffice it to say, perhaps, that the United States has no federally mandated parental leave nor other major legislated benefits facilitating childbearing and child-rearing (Kamerman and Kahn, 1981, 1987; Kamerman et al., 1983). In fact, the United States is the only industrialized nation without some form of statutory maternity leave. Moreover, as Sheila Kamerman points out, "In addition to the obvious lack of child-parenting and family-related benefits at work, employers continue to be unsympathetic and often downright hostile to mothers at the work place" (1980, p. 125).

As for parental leaves, the closest approximation in the United States is the "disability" protection afforded by the 1978 amendments to Title VII of the Civil Rights Act, prohibiting employer discrimination on the basis of pregnancy. And, as noted in Chapter 2, this covers only about 40 percent of American women workers. Though major corporations have begun to address the problem and federal bills on parental leave began to be debated in Congress in 1985, in the United States "being a member of the labor force and a full-time parent means trying to manage against overwhelming odds in an unresponsive society" (Kamerman, 1980, p. 129).

Contrasts

The trends in part-time hours and leaves of absence for Swedish mothers really amplify the issue of time for parenting. Even though over four-

fifths of these mothers are officially in the labor force, they continue to
channel a major portion of their time and energy into home and family,
rather than work. Figure 4.2 casts light on this seeming contradiction. In
1974 over two-fifths of Swedish mothers of young children were out of the
labor force, while over a third were either employed part time or on
leave. Less than a fifth, then, were actually at work 35 hours a week or
more. By 1981 only a fifth remained out of the labor force. What had
changed, however, was not the number employed full time, but the proportion on parental leave and in part-time employment.

Indeed the percentage of mothers of preschoolers who were working at
least 35 hours a week and who were not on leave actually declined from
1974 to 1981, even though the labor force participation rates of this group
increased from 57 to 78 percent. If we look only at those mothers who
were in the labor force (Figure 4.3) we see that the proportional decline
in full-time work was so substantial that by 1981 only one-fifth of preschool mothers in the Swedish labor force were actually on the job full-
time. Thus, the notable changes in roles of Swedish women, in
conjunction with the public policies adopted to assist working parents,
have produced a climate in which parents of young children—thus far it

Figure 4.2. Labor force status of all Swedish mothers of preschoolers (figures for unemployed include self-employed). Source: 1968, 1974, 1981 waves of the Level of Living
Survey, Swedish Institute for Social Research, Stockholm University.

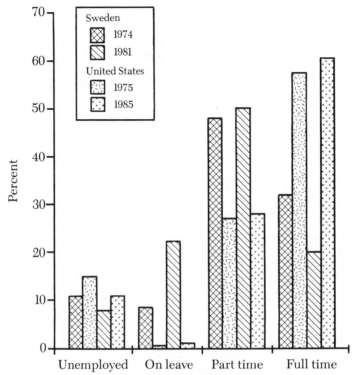

Figure 4.3. Labor force status of Swedish and American mothers of preschoolers in labor force.

Source: For Sweden, 1974, 1981 waves of the Level of Living Survey, Swedish Institute for Social Research, Stockholm University. For the United States, U.S. Bureau of Labor Statistics, 1985.

Note that "unemployed" for Sweden includes women who are self-employed.

has been primarily mothers—have been able to reduce the time actually spent on the job. This finding has important implications for the well-being of employed mothers that will be addressed later.

Comparable data for U.S. mothers are not available, but Figure 4.4 offers a rough estimate of the actual labor force involvement of mothers of preschoolers in the United States for the years 1975 and 1985. The data are imprecise because we do not know exactly how many American mothers (or fathers) may have been on leaves of absence. Using the figure of 40 percent of employed mothers eligible for pregnancy leave in conjunction with the number of mothers of infants in the labor force, we arrive at a probable overestimate of the (minuscule) percentage on leave, as shown in Figures 4.3 and 4.4.

In 1975 over one-fifth of all American mothers with children under six

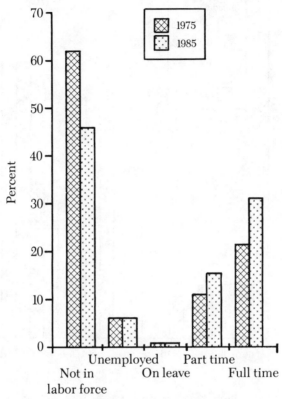

Figure 4.4. Labor force status of all American mothers, 1975, 1985.
  Source: U.S. Bureau of Labor Statistics, 1985.

years of age were employed full time, while over three-fifths were not in
the labor force. By 1985 over half were in the labor force, and nearly a
third were working full time. Looking only at those in the labor force
(Figure 4.3), the proportion working full time increased from 1975 to
1985, and three-fifths of working mothers in 1985 were at work 35 hours
or more per week.

    The United States and Sweden present a study in contrasts quite strik-
ing in its import (see Figure 4.5). Although proportionately fewer mothers of young children in the United States are actually in the labor force,
almost twice as many American mothers are actually at work 35 or more
hours a week. And, unlike Sweden, from the 1970s to the 1980s increasing numbers of American women entered into full-time work. The contrasts between the two countries are dramatic, both with regard to
mothers on leave of absence and those employed part time (Figure 4.5).

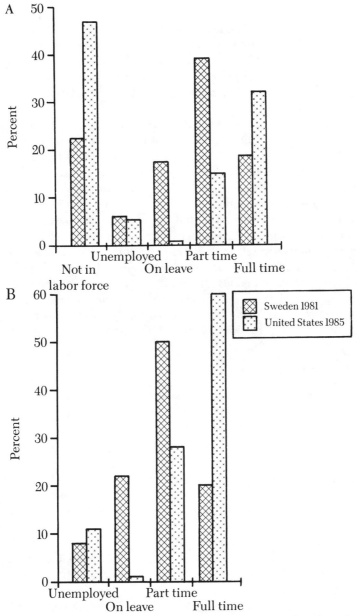

Figure 4.5. Labor force status of Swedish and American mothers. *A*. All mothers. *B*. Mothers of preschoolers in the labor force.

Source: For Sweden, 1981 waves of the Level of Living Survey, Swedish Institute for Social Research, Stockholm University. For the United States, U.S. Bureau of Labor Statistics, 1985.

Note that "unemployed" for Sweden includes women who are self-employed.

Almost two-fifths of all Swedish mothers were working part time in 1981, whereas only 15 percent of American mothers were employed part time four years later. This difference is accounted for in part by differences in the number of homemakers not in the labor force (22 percent in Sweden versus 47 percent in the United States) as well as by the frequency of full-time employment.

Swedish women have been trading full-time homemaking during the early years of child-rearing for part-time employment (Bernhardt, 1987a,b; Sundström, 1987). They have opted for what Bernhardt (1987b) terms a "combination strategy"; they have "one foot in the home and one in the labour market" (p. 9). American women, in contrast, often move from full-time homemaking to full-time employment.

Thus labor force participation in the United States obviously requires mothers to make a greater investment of time than is required in Sweden. Swedish public policies permit working parents to maintain an uninterrupted attachment to the labor force that assures them job seniority and benefit protection, while also allowing them to care for their children during the critical early years. Thus Swedish women can enjoy the benefits of employment during the child-bearing years without paying the typically heavy costs required of employed mothers in the United States.

Physical and Psychological Pressures

To some extent each man or woman puts a personal stamp on the job, but the characteristics of the job are there before the person arrives and they don't change much. (Kahn, 1981, p. 36)

Sweden is justifiably renowned for its efforts to create—through legislation, employer initiative, and collective bargaining—an optimal work climate in which employees play a major role in decisions about the organization and conditions of their work.[1] How have these work reforms that primarily took root in the 1970s affected the work experiences of Swedish parents? Does the quality of their work life vary systematically by gender and by social class, and if so, in what ways?

But first consider how employed mothers and fathers are distributed throughout Sweden's occupational structure. Most striking, though perhaps not surprising, is the fact that fathers are more likely than are mothers to be in higher-level jobs (see Table 4.3). This is, of course, but one illustration of the occupational segregation that pervades all societies and is particularly pronounced in Sweden (Leiniö, 1988). Noteworthy too is

---

1. In particular, these ends were sought through legislative initiatives such as the Codetermination Act of 1977 and the Work Environment Act of 1978.

Table 4.3. Socioeconomic distribution of employed Swedish parents

Occupational level[a]	Fathers (%)			Mothers (%)		
	1968	1974	1981	1968	1974	1981
(N)	(521)	(523)	(446)	(204)	(305)	(390)
Upper	11.5	14.0	14.8	4.8	5.4	6.0
Middle	39.0	35.7	32.6	45.9	48.2	49.4
Working	49.5	50.3	52.5	49.4	46.4	45.6
Total[b]	100	100	99.9	100.1	100	101

Source: 1968, 1974, 1981 waves of the Level of Living Survey, Swedish Institute for Social Research, Stockholm University.

[a]Socioeconomic level is categorized into three groups, with those in professional occupations depicted as upper, white-collar service workers as middle, and manual workers as working.

[b]Totals may not equal 100% because of rounding.

the relative stability of this gender segregation from the late 1960s to the early 1980s, despite the marked influx of women into the labor force and government efforts to reduce segregation in education, training, and employment (Scott, 1982). In 1981 the majority of fathers (53 percent) held working-class jobs, with about 15 percent working as professionals or managers. By contrast, employed mothers were most apt to be in middle-class, white-collar occupations (49 percent in 1981) and only 6 percent held professional jobs. As Wistrand (1981) quips, "In Sweden women and men get paid the same for doing the same jobs. That is why they don't get the same jobs" (p. 53).

Physical Characteristics of Jobs

In examining the employment conditions of working parents in 1968, 1974, and 1981, what is readily apparent are the substantial differences in the demands they made upon men and women (see Table 4.4). Fathers are far more likely than are mothers to be required to lift heavy weights on the job and to perform work that otherwise requires physical exertion. Yet equal proportions of mothers and fathers (about a fifth) describe their jobs as physically exhausting by the end of the work day, even though women's jobs may, by some standards, be less physically demanding.

As would be expected, there are significant differences by occupational level in the physical pressures of the job. Half of the working-class fathers and nearly two-fifths of the working-class mothers are in jobs that require significant physical exertion, and over 60 percent of those in the working class describe their jobs as physically demanding. There are corresponding differences among those who say they feel physically exhausted when

Table 4.4. Working conditions of employed Swedish parents

	Fathers (%)			Mothers (%)		
	1968	1974	1981	1968	1974	1981
(N)	(521)	(523)	(446)	(204)	(305)	(390)
Work demands						
Heavy work	45.8	45.1	39.3	13.5	11.9	12.5
Otherwise physically demanding	42.7	40.9	41.5	43.7	37.4	44.3
Work requiring sweating or physical exertion	33.2	32.7	30.1	20.1	16.1	19.2
Physically exhausting	16.8	16.9	20.8	27.0	20.7	23.0
Mentally strenuous	39.8	40.2	47.0	34.3	33.0	44.5
Hectic work	74.4	68.7	64.4	56.5	57.7	56.6
Monotonous work	15.0	12.9	12.7	20.8	15.4	18.3
Mentally exhausting	13.4	13.6	16.8	19.0	16.4	18.9
Daily work hours						
Works over 9 hr (net)	36.9	25.5	22.2	12.1	12.9	11.6
Works over 8 hr (net)	71.0	46.7	48.3	23.1	25.9	23.2
Works between 6 P.M. and 10 P.M.	26.0	21.1	21.7	27.2	22.8	17.7
Travel time to work exceeds 60 min	30.8	14.4	17.1	21.1	6.6	7.5
Leaves						
Took leave of absence last year	4.1	5.4	6.1	16.2	23.6	30.4
On leave of absence last week[a]	—	1.2	2.0	—	9.2	22.0

Source: 1968, 1974, 1981 waves of the Level of Living Survey, Swedish Institute for Social Research, Stockholm University.
[a]No information for 1968 Survey.

they return home from work; whereas 30 percent of working-class fathers and over 40 percent of working-class mothers say this, only about one in twenty mothers in professional jobs, no fathers who work as professionals, and fewer than one in ten parents (men and women equally) in middle-class occupations report feelings of physical exhaustion.

These findings are clearly supported by my interviews with Swedish parents. Men and women in professional or white-collar jobs rarely mentioned the physical conditions of their work. However, one mother of two preschoolers who worked as a nurse's assistant did describe her job as "a tough job, too little people to help, a heavy work load."

There are other adverse working conditions reported in the Level of Living Survey that differentiate respondents by both class and gender. Working-class parents, especially fathers, are the most likely to experience them: getting dirty on the job; having an awkward or difficult work position; exposure to air pollutants, drafts, noise, dampness, high or low temperatures; and working out of doors. Over half of the parents in working-class occupations, compared to only one in twenty professionals, report that their work often requires repetitive and one-sided movements. Interestingly, women in middle-class occupations are twice as likely to have physically repetitive jobs as are men in this occupational group (38 percent and 19 percent, respectively).

In summary, men and women not only occupy different jobs, but hold jobs that differ considerably in their physical demands. Thus, class as well as gender must be considered in order to accurately portray the physical character of the jobs held by Swedish parents.

Psychological Characteristics of Jobs

Smaller gender differences exist in the psychological demands of employment than in their physical requirements (see Table 4.4). Men are slightly more likely than women to describe their jobs as mentally strenuous or hectic. Women are more apt than men to report their work as monotonous and to describe themselves as feeling mentally exhausted at the end of the working day. In 1981, parents in general were more likely to report their work as mentally strenuous than were parents in 1968 and 1974, suggesting that the psychological stresses of employment for parents had not declined but increased.

Arraying the distribution of psychological strains by occupational level presents a picture different from that portrayed by the distribution of physical demands. Most likely to describe their work as hectic are professional and middle-class fathers: almost three-fourths of them so report, compared to slightly over half of the men in the working class. About three-fifths of all working mothers also depict their jobs as hectic, but this characterization does not vary by occupational class. Large and roughly equal proportions of mothers (72 percent) and fathers (78 percent) who are professionals or managers regard their work as mentally strenuous, compared to much lesser proportions of those in the working class (30 percent of the fathers and 35 percent of the mothers). Over 30 percent of fathers in professional occupations report feeling mentally exhausted when they return home from work, compared to only 10 percent of men in working-class jobs. However, class does not differentiate mothers who find work mentally exhausting.

In interviewing Swedish parents I found that most described the psychological pressures of the job as particularly stressful. One mother of four, a nurse, found it stressful "to be nice, calm, helpful, interested even if you have your own troubles sometimes." Others were likely to report "deadlines" and "time pressures" as stressful. A marketing consultant, a mother of a six-year-old boy, found it difficult "to meet deadlines but do quality work," a problem that was exacerbated when her son got sick. Another mother of a three-year-old said "the most stressful factor affect- ing my and my husband's jobs is when our daughter is getting sick and we're both working on special projects with deadlines." But typically it was fathers, rather than mothers who reported strains from "short deadlines."

In the Level of Living Survey "monotonous work" is the one psycholog- ical strain that is more commonly experienced by working-class parents than those in higher-level occupations and that is more typical of women that men. Over 30 percent of working-class mothers but only one-fifth of working-class fathers report job monotony. None of the parents in profes- sional occupations describe their work as monotonous.

So, as with physical demands, but in different ways, class and gender affect the psychological pressures of employment. Fathers may describe their jobs as more hectic or mentally strenuous, but it is mothers who are most apt to feel mentally exhausted at the day's end. And these feelings of exhaustion are experienced equally among women at all levels in the occupational hierarchy, suggesting that family pressures as well as occupational pressures affect the "mental exhaustion" of working moth- ers (Crouter, 1984).

A U.S. Comparison

There are very few systematically gathered, national data on the condi- tions under which American working parents are employed. From the 1977 Quality of Employment Survey, which provides some information about the characteristics of parents' jobs and how they differ by gender, we find that about a third of the employed mothers and two-fifths of the working fathers of young children say that their work cannot be com- pleted in the allotted time, a condition that could reasonably be depicted as "hectic." And, as in Sweden, more American mothers (67 percent) than fathers (50 percent) say they do repetitious (i.e., monotonous) work (Willer, 1986).

Autonomy and Flexibility

Efforts shall be made to arrange the work so that the employee
himself can influence the work situation. (Swedish Work
Environment Act, 1978)

An important job characteristic is the degree of flexibility and discretion available to workers. Control over one's work schedule and the ability to take time off during the day have been shown to contribute to better synchrony between work and family life (Staines and Pleck, 1983; Nock and Kingston, 1984; Kingston and Nock, 1985). In Sweden one would expect to find a general increase in worker autonomy in the 1970s as a result of the efforts, by legislation and collective bargaining, to achieve greater workplace democracy by changing traditional institutional decision-making practices (Swedish Institute, 1983).

Information about various discretionary behaviors on the job reveals significant gender differences in the degree of workplace autonomy (see Table 4.5). For example, in 1981 mothers of young children were somewhat more likely than fathers to accept private phone calls at work (91 to 81 percent), but fathers were slightly more able to receive visitors on the job (86 to 78 percent). But over a third of the fathers were required to use time clocks in 1981, a constraint imposed on less than a fourth of the employed mothers.

The largest gender difference also marks the greatest single change over the thirteen-year study period: the ability to leave the workplace for about a half-hour without notifying a superior. Nearly three-fifths of the fathers were able to do so in 1981, compared to fewer than half in 1968. For mothers, however, this entitlement hardly changed at all from 1968 to 1981. Finally, in 1981 an important new question regarding flexible working hours was introduced in the Level of Living Survey, with the interesting result that nearly half of the fathers reported themsleves to be on flexible schedules, compared to but one-third of the mothers.

Table 4.5. Workplace constraints and freedoms of employed Swedish parents

	Fathers (%)			Mothers (%)		
	1968	1974	1981	1968	1974	1981
(N)	(521)	(523)	(446)	(204)	(305)	(390)
Workplace particular about hours	70.0	69.4	62.4	68.2	70.0	73.0
Have to use time clock	34.6	36.3	35.1	15.6	18.9	23.8
Can receive private phone calls	75.0	81.4	83.3	71.5	82.1	91.2
Can make private phone calls	88.3	91.7	92.0	81.4	84.3	91.2
Can leave for 30 min without telling superior	46.3	50.8	58.2	26.0	27.5	29.5
Can receive private visits	79.1	82.3	86.0	65.3	71.6	77.6

Source: 1968, 1974, 1981 waves of the Level of Living Survey, Swedish Institute for Social Research, Stockholm University.

In my own interviews I found job autonomy frequently cited as a way of reducing the strains of balancing work and family roles. A self-employed translator who worked out of his home and who was the father of a six-year-old son valued the flexibility in "setting my own working hours." And his wife, employed full time, found that the flexibility introduced when her husband started his own business improved her own life as well.

Data from the Level of Living Survey reveal that, as might have been anticipated, job constraints and freedoms are closely related to occupational level, but not always in the expected direction. To be sure, working-class jobs most commonly require punctuality and seldom permit employees to take time off during the day. However, some other differences by occupational position are not easily interpreted. For example, men and women in middle-class jobs are more likely than those either above or below them to be able to receive private visits during working hours. Surprising, too, is the absence of a statistically significant difference among social classes—and hence among broad occupational groups—in the requirement that a time clock be used.

The U.S. Quality of Employment Survey includes one question that corresponds to a query in the Swedish Level of Living Survey, concerning the ability to take time off for family or personal reasons. About equal proportions of employed American mothers and fathers of preschoolers had this flexibility in 1977 (36.7 percent and 39.3 percent respectively—see Willer, 1986). Compare this finding with that from Sweden, where in 1981 over 58 percent of the fathers (but only 29 percent of the mothers) could easily leave the job for a half-hour without reporting to anyone.

Other Employment Characteristics

We know that women are much less likely than men to hold upper-level professional jobs, and we have seen thus far that women's employment conditions are also considerably different from those of men, whether one looks at working time and schedules or the physical and psychological characteristics of jobs. We have seen too that both men and women in working-class jobs have quite different employment experiences than do those at the middle and upper occupational levels. Still another difference by occupational level and gender is the degree of supervisory responsibility exercised. Nearly two-thirds of the male professionals report having at least one subordinate, a responsibility held by only 14 percent of the fathers and 8 percent of the mothers in working-class jobs. But particularly interesting is the finding that relatively few women even in upper-level occupations (27 percent) report that they have a super-visory role. This underscores the notion that men and women, even pro-fessionals, occupy different jobs, with men typically higher in the occupational hierarchy.

Still another important dimension of employment experience in Swe-den is union participation. Women are traditionally less likely than men to be actively involved in union affairs, but from 1968 to 1981 mem-bership and levels of union participation changed for both men and women (see Table 4.6). It is clear that the gender differences in union involvement progressively narrowed over that twelve-year period. Although men remain more actively involved in their unions than do women (at least those with young children), the percentage of women holding union office increased more than five-fold and the proportion otherwise active in union affairs nearly doubled during this period.

The extent of union membership in Sweden markedly contrasts with that of workers in the United States, where only 27 percent of all eligible men and 11 percent of all eligible women in the labor force are union members (Freeman and Medoff, 1984). The widespread unionization of the Swedish work force has enabled the great majority of workers to bar-gain collectively with employers and to see themselves, and to be seen, not merely as individuals but as members of a group with common inter-ests, concerns and aims (Korpi, 1982; Ruggie, 1984). The strength of Swedish unionism as reflected in union membership has provided a major impetus for the adoption of public policies promoting the interests of working parents.

Table 4.6. Union involvement of employed Swedish parents

Union activities	Fathers (%)			Mothers (%)		
	1968	1974	1981	1968	1974	1981
(*N*)	(521)	(523)	(446)	(204)	(305)	(390)
Not a member	24.1	20.2	10.5	51.8	40.3	15.7
Member, not active	39.2	37.0	35.8	34.2	36.9	45.9
Active, not on committees	19.9	23.3	27.1	10.6	16.1	20.9
Officer, on committees	16.6	19.4	26.5	3.4	6.6	17.5
Total[a]	99.8	99.9	99.9	100	99.9	100

Source: 1968, 1974, 1981 waves of the Level of Living Survey, Swedish Institute for Social Research, Stockholm University.

[a]Totals may not equal 100% because of rounding.

Employment Insecurity

A system may adjust well to small disruptions, yet a major crisis
will send it into violent and prolonged fluctuations. An auto-
matic pilot may be able to cope with any normal gusts of wind
and maintain the aeroplane on a stable course. Nevertheless
there will be situations that warrant the intervention of a human
pilot. (Faxén, 1982, p. 182)

There is no more important issue for families than the stability of parents'
employment. An impressive body of literature has documented convincingly the deleterious effects of job loss on workers and their children (see
review by Moen et al., 1983). There is evidence, at least in the United
States, that parents of young children are particularly vulnerable to job
loss, given their relatively limited seniority and job experience (Moen,
1983; Pearlin et al., 1981). Is this vulnerability also common to Swedish
men and women in their childbearing years? With its strong valuation of
job security and its deep commitment to full employment, manifested in
the 1974 Security of Employment Act and Promotion of Employment
Act, as well as the Codetermination Act of 1977, Sweden has succeeded
in holding down unemployment across the board (see Table 4.7) despite
the vagaries of the world economy and the business cycle (Leighton and
Gustafsson, 1984; Ginsberg, 1983; Swedish Institute, 1983). Given this
commitment to minimizing the individual and social costs of unemployment, did the situation of parents of young children change during the
1970s?

One of the inadvertent consequences of adopting a policy of relatively
permanent employment, safeguarding workers against dismissal, has
been a counter-trend toward increasing the number of jobs defined as

Table 4.7. Job insecurity of employed Swedish parents

Job status	Fathers (%)			Mothers (%)		
	1968	1974	1981	1968	1974	1981
(N)	(521)	(523)	(446)	(204)	(305)	(390)
Unemployed at any time in last 5 years	10.5	14.7	8.2	7.5	17.6	7.8
Current job perceived as temporary	2.3	2.5	5.9	3.4	3.4	5.9

Source: 1968, 1974, 1981 waves of the Level of Living Survey, Swedish Institute for Social
Research, Stockholm University.

Note: These unemployment rates (for a 5-year period) for parents are somewhat higher
than those for Swedish men and women generally. For men aged 16–74, the unemployment
rate was 2.0 in 1968, 2.2 in 1973, and 1.7 in 1980. For women, rates were 2.3, 2.8, and 2.3 in
1967, 1973, and 1980, respectively (Leighton and Gustafsson, 1984, p. 277).

"temporary" and therefore not subject to the strictures governing more permanent jobs (Leighton and Gustafsson, 1984). This increase in temporary or "part-period" work can also be seen as an employer response to parental leave and other family policies which frequently produce a need for temporary workers. And indeed, there has been a steady increase in the numbers of both sexes holding temporary jobs. Nearly 6 percent of working parents in 1981 expected their jobs to end in the near future. Thus, joblessness per se did not change in Sweden from 1968 to 1981, but impermanent work grew. There are no identical data on American parents, but in 1977 only about a third of the respondents in a national sample of working parents of young children described their jobs as secure (Willer, 1986).

Conclusions

As long as husband and wife are unequal in the labor market, they will inevitably be unequal at home; on average, the one who contributes less by employment will contribute more at home. (Davis, 1984, p. 413)

In summary, what can be said about the employment conditions of working parents in Sweden? It is most noteworthy that, despite the efforts of the labor movement and the Social Democratic Party (its principal political ally) to reduce class- and gender-based inequalities, mothers and fathers, as well as different occupational classes, have quite different employment conditions and experiences. Changes in public policies leading to reduced working hours and mandating parental leaves of absence undeniably enabled women to accommodate work to family roles, but they produced very little change in the work involvement of fathers. These policies for working parents, *however*, have permitted women to maintain their labor force attachment while starting a family and simultaneously to take time off from work during the early years of child-rearing by means of paid leaves of absence and part-time schedules.

The differentiation of function between men and women that is so characteristic of family life is isomorphic with the division of labor we see in work life. For example, men are more likely than are women to be engaged in physical labor and to supervise subordinates, while women are more likely to have jobs where they perform monotonous tasks. Mothers and fathers may well share the family role of economic provider in that both are apt to be in the labor force, but they surely do not perform the same jobs or play the same occupational roles, even in Sweden.

Neither do parents, men or women, at different occupational levels experience similar work environments. Psychologically demanding work is more characteristic of professional occupations and physically gruelling activity more typical of working-class jobs.

Beyond the overall increase in the labor force participation of mothers and the related increases in their part-time employment and in leave-taking, the 1968–81 trend data analyzed fail to reveal any other truly striking changes in the day-to-day job realities of Swedish mothers and fathers during this period, despite the campaign for work environment reform and industrial democracy that was launched in the 1970s. Still, public policy changes have played a vital role in facilitating women's employment. It is in large measure by availing themselves of various legislated options (parental leaves and part-time employment) that Swedish women are able to continue in the labor force during the early and most demanding years of childbearing and child-rearing. American mothers, by contrast, typically move in and out of employment, in and out of part-time work while seeking a satisfactory balance between work and family obligations (Moen, 1985).

Research has consistently demonstrated how experiences on the job spill over into family life. (Kohn, 1977, 1987; Piotrkowski, 1979; Crouter and Perry-Jenkins, 1986). A broad ecological perspective would hold that the conditions of parents' employment affects the lives of their children in both direct and indirect ways (Bronfenbrenner and Crouter, 1983; Kamerman and Hayes, 1982). For example, the number and scheduling of working hours directly determine the extent to which mothers and fathers have the *opportunity* to parent. The wide variations by gender and class in working conditions documented in this chapter indicate that the effects of work on parenting would differ markedly between Swedish mothers and fathers as well as among parents occupying different positions in the occupational hierarchy. The gender and class differences in well-being reported in Chapter 3 may well reflect differential exposure to stressful conditions of work. The following chapter examines the contribution of these job experiences to parental well-being.

5

Working Conditions and Well-Being

It is critical to bridge the gap between knowledge of the stress-producing aspects of work situations and family systems. How tension and illness-producing features of one system affect the likelihood of a member's successful adjustment to the other is important to know, especially if we are able to extend our understanding of these barriers to well-being in our society. (Kanter, 1977, p. 81)

Chapter 3 reported, using time-series analyses, that the well-being of Swedish mothers improved from 1968 to 1981. What accounts for this lessening of their psychological distress and fatigue, especially among those doing "double duty" in the labor force and in the home? I suggest that the answer lies in the new public policies adopted during this period which gave working parents—but particularly mothers—more options and more flexibility in apportioning their time between the workplace and the home.

In Chapter 4, I described some major variations in the work environments of Swedish parents, differences by both gender and location in the occupational hierarchy. This chapter develops the implications of these findings for parental well-being. I first examine the relationship between women's labor force involvement and their reported psychological distress and fatigue and then go on to explore possible linkages between various employment conditions and changes in their well-being.

Well-Being and the Labor Force Attachments of Mothers

The pressure for change in the organization of work and family life will persist, and some form of social change is assured, but change will not necessarily lessen the dilemmas women face. (Gerson, 1985, p. 223)

I have several times noted the striking increase in the proportion of mothers of preschoolers in the Swedish labor force from 1968 to 1981; here, I address some implications of this social trend. Does maternal employment lead to psychological strain and fatigue or, conversely, does it contribute to feelings of well-being? Have the effects of employment become more pronounced over this time? Do employed mothers in the early 1980s react differently to their circumstances from those who were in the labor force in the late 1960s? Still a third issue, in keeping with a life course perspective, is the consequence of *transitions* into and out of the labor force for psychological well-being.

In Chapter 2 I noted that social scientists investigating the relationships between employment and mental health in women had arrived at conflicting conclusions. Is the historical differentiation of function between mothers and fathers in industrial societies an important mechanism for precluding conflicting occupational and family demands, so that parents in traditional roles seldom experience role conflict or overload? Or has the isolation of women within the home contributed to psychological distress by effectively cutting them off from sources of power, prestige, and adult social relations?

One possible explanation for the inconsistent findings is that such research generally fails to consider the age and life stage of the women being studied. In particular, it has seldom targeted an important subgroup of women: mothers of young children. Mothers with infants and toddlers are the group most vulnerable to role overload and strain, and they may derive the least benefit from assuming the additional role of worker (see Radloff, 1975; Cleary and Mechanic, 1983; Wethington, 1987).

Yet these mothers are also prone to social isolation, as a result of their heavy involvement in child-rearing. As Gavron observed (1966), "The mother at home with young children is isolated from the main stream of society. In a work oriented society, those who do not work have some reduction in status, and housewives, no matter how arduous housework actually proves to be, do not feel themselves to be at work" (p. 146). Thus the contrary argument: that mothers of preschoolers might well be expected to benefit from paid employment.

The findings presented in Chapter 3 suggest that increased maternal employment in Sweden has had a salutary effect on women's well-being. But this otherwise straightforward conclusion is complicated by the fact that the labor force participation of Swedish mothers of young children often means part-time employment and being on leaves of absence. Accordingly, the links between maternal employment and well-being require more careful scrutiny.

Social Change in Employment and Well-Being

The distribution of maternal well-being by survey year, location in the socioeconomic structure, and labor force status are presented in Table 5.1. There indeed was a progressive decline from 1968 to 1981 in the proportions of employed women in the labor force with symptoms of psychological strain, with the greatest decrease occurring among women in upper-level, professional jobs. Moreover, there was also a corresponding decrease in the proportions of employed women reporting fatigue over the three survey periods. But for those not in the labor force there was an increase in the proportion of working-class women reporting psychological distress.

It seems, therefore, that the effects of employment may have changed from 1968 to 1981. Being a working mother in 1968, when there were comparatively few women with young children in the labor force and fewer legislated supports for working parents, apparently was more stressful than the experience of employment in 1981, under a new set of conditions.

Table 5.1. Well-being of Swedish mothers by socioeconomic[a] and labor force status

| Measures of well-being | Mothers (%) | | | | | |
| | In labor force | | | Not in labor force | | |
	1968	1974	1981	1968	1974	1981
(N)	(204)	(305)	(390)	(359)	(225)	(111)
Psychological strains[b]						
Upper	55.9**	31.8**	9.1**	28.8	16.7	40.6[c]
Middle	31.1	29.8	23.2	35.0	33.6	24.9
Working	39.1	37.4	28.1	29.8*	43.4*	36.0*
All mothers	36.1**	33.4**	24.6**	32.0	37.7	33.1
Daily fatigue[d]						
Upper	55.9	31.5	36.2	32.1	49.3	40.6
Middle	43.6+	44.3+	35.2+	47.2	40.1	44.8
Working	56.7	47.7	47.3	48.5	55.4	47.9
All mothers	50.7+	45.2+	40.8+	47.1	48.9	47.1

Source: 1968, 1974, 1981 waves of the Level of Living Survey, Swedish Institute for Social Research, Stockholm University.

[a]Socioeconomic level is categorized into three groups, with those in professional occupations depicted as upper, white-collar service workers as middle, and manual workers as lower. Women who are not in the labor force are classified on the basis of previous occupation.

[b]Percent in each category reporting symptoms of psychological strain over the past 12 months.

[c]N for this group in 1981 only 9.

[d]Percent in each category reporting daily fatigue over past two weeks.

Difference by year: $+p < .10$; $*p < .05$; $**p < .01$.

But charting broad trends in the well-being of Swedish mothers from 1968 to 1974 tells us nothing of changes in the well-being of individual women as they move through their childbearing and child-rearing years, and as they move in and out of the labor force. To examine the effects of these experiences I track women across two surveys: the 1968–74 and the 1974–81 cohorts, respectively. Each sample consists of women who either had preschoolers in the home or became mothers during these periods.

The relationships between labor force attachment and the two measures of women's well-being, psychological distress and daily fatigue, are illustrated by the data in Figure 5.1. Looking first at psychological strain, we see both consistency and variability in the data for 1968–74 and 1974–81. In the 1968–74 cohort, those who left the labor force before 1974 (i.e., who were employed in 1968 only) were the most apt to experience strain in 1974; nearly two-fifths of them reported it. However, there is no statistically significant difference by *current* employment status (for the 1968–74 cohort, in 1974) in the proportions reporting strain; women out of the labor force reported no more nor less psychological distress than those who were employed. In 1981 employment seems to have been more closely related to well-being; those moving into the labor force in this year, as well as those employed in both 1974 and 1981, were the *least likely* to report psychological strain.

Turning to the prevalence of fatigue (Figure 5.1b), we find that again it is those in both the 1968–74 and 1974–81 cohorts who had *left* the labor force who were most likely to report daily tiredness. Employed mothers were slightly less likely to report fatigue in 1974 and 1981 than were women not in the labor force.

The data presented in Figure 5.1 appear to confirm what is hinted at in Chapter 3 and apparent in the time-series trends—that employment became somewhat less trying for members of the 1974–81 cohort than for those in the 1968–74 cohort. There is an 8-percentage-point difference in reports of psychological strain among those who were employed in both 1968 and 1974 and those working in both 1974 and 1981 (34.1 percent versus 26.4 percent). Moreover, there is a 6-percentage-point difference in reported distress of those who moved into the labor force; new entrants in 1981 were less likely to experience strain than were new entrants in 1974. The most distressed by 1981 appear to be those not in the labor force and others who left after entering it. Once again, this is particularly true of working-class women; over 40 percent of those not in the labor force in 1981 reported symptoms of distress, compared to a fourth of those in the upper and middle classes. Notable too is the fact that a smaller proportion of women in every labor force category reported daily fatigue in 1981 than in 1974.

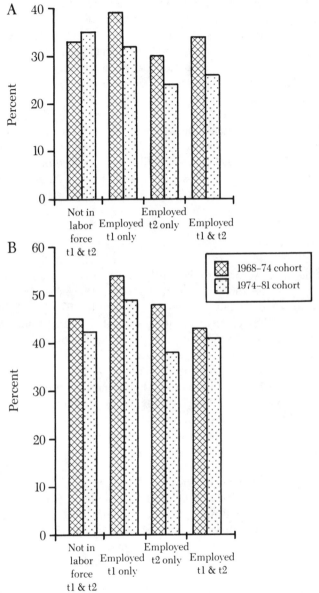

Figure 5.1. Employment and well-being of Swedish mothers. *A*. Percentage reporting psychological strain. *B*. Percentage reporting daily fatigue. t1 is 1968 for 1968–74 cohort, 1974 for 1974–81 cohort. t2 is 1974 for 1968–74 cohort, 1981 for 1974–81 cohort.

Source: 1968, 1974, 1981 waves of the Level of Living Survey, Swedish Institute for Social Research, Stockholm University.

But the data in Figure 5.1, while accurately describing the distribution of distress symptoms across various subgroups, do not necessarily establish a causal relationship between labor force attachment per se and well-being. For example, one unresolved issue is the impact of *initial* distress and fatigue on *subsequent* employment. Women with high levels of psychological distress may well be the ones most likely to remain out of or to leave the labor force.

An examination of the data on early reports of fatigue and strain suggests that there is indeed a statistically significant, though modest, relationship between initial level of well-being and subsequent employment experience. Women who reported either high fatigue or psychological distress in 1974 were slightly less likely than those who did not report such symptoms to be employed in 1981.[1]

Multivariate Analysis

Multiple regression estimates including a variety of individual and family variables, as well as initial level of well-being, suggest that employment per se only slightly affects psychological strain or daily fatigue: (1) for the 1968–74 cohort of women, those entering the labor force by 1974 were likely to report less strain in 1974 (see Table 5.2); (2) for the 1974–81 cohort, employment status had a slight effect on fatigue (but not psychological strain)—those leaving the labor force by 1981 were the most likely to experience additional fatigue in 1981.

But even though maternal employment does not by itself directly influence well-being in any major way, there could be interaction effects involving employment status. In other words, perhaps it is only under certain conditions that employment has a bearing on women's psychological health. Among the factors that may moderate the effect of employment are stage of the life-cycle, marital status, previous level of well-being, and social class.

To detect these possible interactions, log linear models were tested for both the 1968–74 and 1974–81 cohorts. The models include both current (time 2, t2) and prior (time 1, t1) employment status. Controlling for various contextual factors, it becomes clear that employment in itself does not make a statistically significant contribution to the estimation of psychological distress for either cohort of women.

1. To establish possible causal links between employment status and well-being requires the construction and testing of multivariate models that take into account the influence of other pertinent and potentially confounding factors, such as initial level of well-being. Of those with low fatigue in 1974, 84 percent were employed in 1981, compared to 78 percent of those with high fatigue; 84 percent of those reporting symptoms of psychological strain in 1974 were employed in 1981, compared to 77 percent of those without such symptoms. Both differences are statistically significant.

Table 5.2. Likelihood of fatigue and psychological distress for Swedish mothers, 1974 and 1981 (metric coefficients)

	Fatigue[a]		Strain[b]	
	1974	1981	1974	1981
(*N*)	(305)	(390)	(305)	(390)
Employed t1 and t2[c]	.054	.045	−.014	.003
Employed t1 only	−.021	.114[+]	−.015	−.053
Employed t2 only	.006	.012	−.089[*]	−.090

Source: 1968, 1974, 1981 waves of the Level of Living Survey, Swedish Institute for Social Research, Stockholm University.

Notes: Respondents are included in the first cohort if they either had a preschooler in 1968 or became a parent by 1974. Similarly respondents in the 1974–81 cohort either had a preschooler in 1974 or became a parent by 1981. Controls include age, life stage, education, and previous (t1) levels of strain and fatigue.

[a]Guttman scale of reported fatigue over last two weeks.

[b]Guttman scale of reported symptoms of psychological distress over past year.

[c]t1 represents 1968 for 1968–74 cohort and 1974 for 1974–81 cohort; t2 represents 1974 for the 1968–74 cohort and 1981 for the 1974–81 cohort. Out of the labor force both t1 and t2 is the omitted category.

[+]$p < .10$; [*]$p < .05$.

However, for women in the 1968–74 cohort, employment does make a difference in the estimation of daily fatigue. Those who left the labor force between 1968 and 1974 were the most likely to express feelings of tiredness in 1974 (controlling for previous fatigue as well as marital status and social class). There is, moreover, an interaction between employment experience and previous fatigue (see Figure 5.2), in that those who entered the labor force between 1968 and 1974 and who had not in 1968 reported fatigue were even *less likely* to report fatigue in 1974 than any other group of women. By contrast, those who reported fatigue in 1968 and entered the labor force by 1974 were more likely to report it in 1974. But this relationship between employment status and previous symptoms of fatigue fails to hold for the 1974–81 cohort, suggesting that labor force participation per se may have become a less central factor in the experience of fatigue in the 1980s than it was in the middle 1970s.

What about the effects of a wife's employment on her *husband's* well-being? Some researchers (Moore and Sawhill, 1978; Kessler and McRae, 1982; Burke and Weir, 1976) suggest that husbands with employed wives may be at a psychological and career disadvantage compared to men whose wives accept full-time responsibility for home and family. On the other hand, a husband who participates in family life as a consequence of his wife's employment may enhance his own feelings of well-being (Pleck, 1985; Kessler and McRae, 1982; Baruch and Barnett, 1986). Or, for that matter, men may be unaffected by their wives' employment, absorbed, as it were, in their own careers.

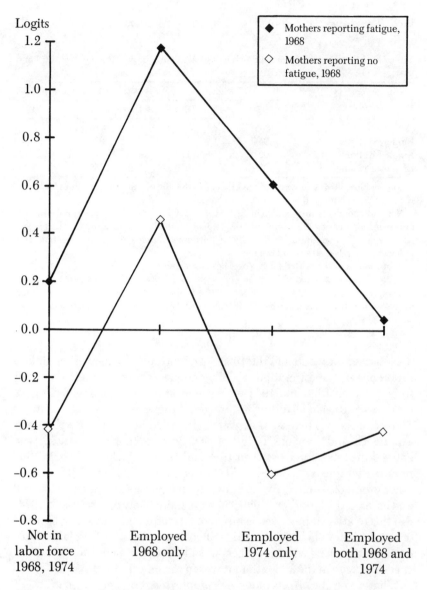

Logits

Not in labor force 1968, 1974 | Employed 1968 only | Employed 1974 only | Employed both 1968 and 1974

◆ Mothers reporting fatigue, 1968
◇ Mothers reporting no fatigue, 1968

Effect parameters (lambdas) of logit model controlling for marital status and social class

Model is WXF MF CF WXMCS (G^2 = 90.49, d.f. = 62, p = .045, N = 716)

Figure 5.2. Likelihood of Swedish mothers experiencing fatigue, 1974, by work experience and previous fatigue. C = social class (upper and middle, working), F = daily fatigue (no, yes), M = marital status (married/cohabiting, not married/cohabiting), S = family stage (new mothers, preschoolers both years, middle childhood), W = employment (working, not working), X = previous fatigue (no, yes).

Source: 1968, 1974 waves of the Level of Living Survey, Swedish Institute for Social Research, Stockholm University.

Looking first at symptoms of psychological distress, we find that in 1981 reports of strain by fathers of young children are unrelated to their wives' labor force participation, once the demands of their own jobs and their previous level of strain are taken into account. However, the employment of wives does have an impact on the daily fatigue experienced by their husbands in 1981, although it interacts with the latter's previous (in 1974) level of fatigue (see Figure 5.3). Thus, those husbands

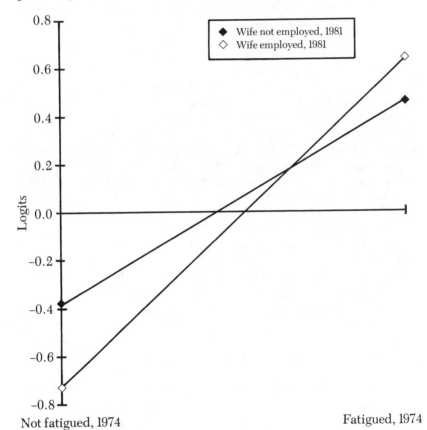

Effect parameters (lambdas) of logit model controlling for family stage, job autonomy, and job demands

Model is FWX FDA FS SDWAX ($G^2 = 71.80$, d.f. $= 54$, $p = .053$, $N = 644$)

Figure 5.3. Likelihood of Swedish fathers experiencing fatigue, 1981, by wife's employment status and previous fatigue. A = job autonomy, D = job demands, F = daily fatigue (no, yes), S = family stage (new fathers, preschoolers both years, middle childhood), W = employment (working, not working), X = previous fatigue (no, yes).

Source: 1974, 1981 waves of the Level of Living Survey, Swedish Institute for Social Research, Stockholm University.

who did not report high fatigue in 1974 and whose wives were employed in 1981 were less likely to report tiredness than those whose wives were not in the labor force. Conversely, men who already reported fatigue in 1974 were more likely to report it again in 1981 if their wives were employed.

What do the data reveal about the relationship between maternal employment and the well-being of Swedish parents? First, being in the labor force became less stressful for working mothers from 1968 to 1981. In 1968, when there were few legislated supports available and comparatively few mothers of young children were employed, working mothers were more likely than those not in the labor force to report symptoms of psychological strain over the previous twelve months. But in 1974 and 1981 it was the nonworking mothers who were more likely to report such symptoms. Given the strong social insurance incentives (such as parental leave and part-time employment) for combining employment and motherhood (Sundström, 1987), the Swedish women who remained full-time homemakers may have become an increasingly select and socially marginal group. By 1981 over four-fifths of mothers of young children were in the labor force, braced by a number of legislated forms of assistance.

Second, knowing a woman's employment status does not provide enough information to predict whether she will experience psychological distress or feelings of fatigue. Working very probably entails both costs and benefits, as does staying out of the labor force; whether the balance-sheet favored one over the other in Sweden in 1981 is not at all clear. What must be considered are the conditions both at home and at work. These are especially important in light of the fact that changes in well-being from 1968 to 1981 did not occur uniformly across all socioeconomic levels; lowered levels of stress were most pronounced for women in professional occupations.

And finally, the fact of his wife's employment actually *reduces* the likelihood that a father of young children, with no previous experience of fatigue, will report daily fatigue in 1981, although it increases the likelihood that those with previous fatigue will continue to report it in 1981.

These findings undercut the belief that maternal employment *necessarily* contributes to the strains and overloads or, conversely, to the well-being of either parent. They are consistent, on the other hand, with the more recent views which underscore the complexity of the relationship between employment and emotional health (Warr and Perry, 1982; Ross et al., 1983; Mirowsky and Ross, 1986; Kessler and McRae, 1984; Thoits, 1983; Wethington, 1987). These findings suggest, moreover, that the differences between Swedish mothers in and out of paid employment have become less marked and that factors *other than employment status per se* account for changes in individual well-being. So let us now examine the explanatory power of some other factors—specifically, conditions of work.

Working Hours, Leaves of Absence, and Well-Being

It is the loss of free time accompanying parenthood that sur-
prises and bothers new parents more than anything else. The
scarcity of this valued resource creates a conflict of interest
between husbands and wives. (LaRossa and LaRossa, 1981,
p. 46)

Critical to the emotional health and energy level of parents may not be employment per se but specific features of the job situation. For working parents in the United States, a crucial contribution to work–family conflicts and overloads is the total number of hours spent at work each week (Keith and Schafer, 1980; Pleck et al., 1980; Bohen and Viveros-Long, 1981; Willer, 1986; Galinsky, 1987). Shift work and otherwise inconvenient hours also have been shown to be associated with parental stress (Lein et al., 1974; Pleck and Staines, 1985).

One strategy for resolving the role overload of employed parents involves reducing the amount of time spent on the job. In Sweden possible attenuators of psychological strain and fatigue are two legislated benefits: the options of part-time work and parental leaves of absence.

We have seen, in Chapter 4, that part-time work is the preferred employment choice of the majority of Swedish mothers of young children. But although in 1981 fully two-thirds of mothers in the labor force were employed less than full time (i.e., less than 35 hours a week), there is no statistically significant difference between the percentages of part- and full-timers reporting symptoms of psychological distress, at least at the bivariate level (see Table 5.3). There is, however, such a difference for shift workers; more women on shifts evidence strain than those working regular daytime hours. Of the women on evening, night, or early morning shifts nearly two-fifths reported symptoms of distress. Yet there is no corresponding, statistically significant difference by shift in the distress experienced by fathers, perhaps reflecting the fact that mothers do double duty at home and at work whereas fathers continue to concentrate primarily on their jobs.

Daily fatigue, the second measure of well-being, is related to working hours in 1981, with women on part-time schedules the least likely to

Table 5.3. Work involvement and well-being of employed Swedish parents, 1981

	Fathers (% reporting)[a]		Mothers (% reporting)	
	Psychological strain	Daily fatigue	Psychological strain	Daily fatigue
Leave of absence (last week)[b]				
On leave	—	—	26.9	35.8+
Not on leave	—	—	25.4	41.9+
Work hours				
Part time	36.1+	52.2+	22.8	36.2**
Full time	15.5+	31.9+	27.5	48.9**
Shift work				
Regular day	16.7	32.6*	21.5*	19.3+
Night, evening, or early morning	18.2	51.6*	37.9*	25.0+
Two or more shifts	20.9	34.6*	33.1*	48.2+
Irregular shifts	7.4	18.4*	41.9*	22.8+

Source: 1981 wave of the Level of Living Survey, Swedish Institute for Social Research, Stockholm University.

[a]N = 446 for fathers, 390 for mothers.

[b]Less than 2 percent of fathers were on leave the preceding week.

+p < .10; *p < .05; **p < .01.

report fatigue. Fathers working part time, on the other hand, are more likely to report fatigue and distress, possibly as a reaction to involuntary reductions in their working hours. Fatigue is also associated with shift work for both mothers and fathers. Those who have regular daytime hours are significantly less likely to report feeling tired.

What does a parental leave of absence mean for the psychological well-being of working parents? Since this is an option elected by so few fathers (fewer than 2 percent of those in the 1981 sample reported being on leave the week prior to the study), it is impossible to gauge the significance of parental leaves for their emotional strain or fatigue. However, in 1981 the 17 percent of employed mothers who were on leave the previous week had levels of well-being similar to those actually on the job at the time, being neither less tired nor experiencing less psychological strain. In their investigation of first-time mothers, Moen and Forest (1989) found that being on a leave of absence did reduce the likelihood of psychological strain. The parental leave issue, of course, is confounded with childbearing, since those with infants are the most likely to be on leave. And, since virtually all Swedish children under one year of age are cared for by their parents, there is no comparison group of mothers who continue on the job during their child's first year.

Multivariate Analysis

How do working hours and leaves of absence affect parental well-being once other potentially confounding factors are controlled? After all, it may not be the hours at work but conditions in the home that contribute to distress and fatigue (Crouter, 1984). For example, one mother I interviewed, in describing her morning routine of getting the whole family up, dressed, and fed, said she felt exhausted by the time she arrived at work. So perhaps it is family demands—or the fact of being a single parent—that most influence well-being. Accordingly, multivariate regression equations including a number of individual, family, and occupational measures (listed in Appendix B) were estimated. These analyses reveal that part-time schedules did have a mitigating effect on women's feelings of daily fatigue in 1981, even after taking a range of other factors into account (see Table 5.4). However, neither psychological strain nor daily fatigue proved to have a direct relationship to leaves of absence when the same controls were applied.

Interestingly, for the 1974-81 cohort, and again controlling for other factors, men whose wives work part time are less likely to report increased psychological distress. But men's own working hours and schedules apparently have no direct effects on either their psychological strain or fatigue. This again suggests that fathers as well as mothers see family work as essentially "women's work"; where women can successfully manage both their work and family roles, for example, through part-time employment, both parents benefit.

Log linear analyses, applied to explore possible interaction effects in predicting the likelihood of psychological strains for the 1974-81 cohort of employed mothers, reveal that, after controlling for job demands and previous psychological strains, being on leave or working part-time hours do not significantly contribute to the estimation of strain in 1981. However (again after controlling for job demands), employed mothers who were working fewer than 35 hours a week or on parental leave were less likely to report fatigue in 1981 if they did not report it in 1974. (These circumstances, did not, however, influence the 1981 outcome for those who had reported fatigue in 1974.) For employed mothers who reported no fatigue in 1974 and who in 1981 were working full time, not on leave, the odds were 1.33 to 1 that they reported fatigue in 1981. In contrast, women who reported no fatigue in 1974 but who in 1981 were either working part-time hours or were on leave had only a .75 to 1 chance of reporting fatigue—again controlling for demands of the job.

If reduced working hours make it easier to juggle work and parenting,

Table 5.4. Likelihood of psychological strain and daily fatigue for employed Swedish parents (metric coefficients)

	Fathers				Mothers			
	Fatigue[a]		Strain[b]		Fatigue		Strain	
	1974	1981	1974	1981	1974	1981	1971	1981
(N)	(678)	(676)	(678)	(676)	(487)	(575)	(487)	(575)
Working hours and scheduling								
Part-time hours	.047	.002	-.008	.041	-.063	-.149*	-.051	-.061
Overtime	-.007	.019	-.029	.044	.097*	.023	.026	-.057
Shiftwork	-.011	-.049	-.013	-.008	.125**	.121**	.050	.054
Leave last week	-.037	-.033	-.061	.046	.011	-.015	.070	.002
Leave last year	.003	.019	.049	.018	-.017	.009	.034	.023
Spouse full-time	.062	.004	.023	.031	—	—	—	—
Spouse part-time	-.007	-.016	-.042	-.082*	-.040	-.014	-.031	-.011
Spouse overtime	.020	.028	.007	.016	.005	.001	.087+	.074+
Working environment								
Physical pressures								
t1[c]	.041	-.026	-.022	.064	-.082	.070	-.042	.071
t2	.080+	.090*	.077+	-.053	.074	-.026	-.054	-.031
Psychological pressures								
t1	-.037	.020	-.040	.029	-.020	.061	.057	.035
t2	.130**	.119**	.078+	.129**	.088+	.128**	.082+	.098*
Occupational level								
Upper	-.024	.078*	.075	.125**	-.077	.035	.051	-.080+
Working	-.016	.103*	.007	.123**	.012	-.058	.100	.067
Spouse–upper					-.077	-.013	-.060	.037
Spouse–working					-.069	.003	-.032	-.001
Self-direction								
Autonomy	-.026	-.083*	-.021	-.028	-.025	-.056	.012	-.053
Sets own pace		.046		.023		.033		.011
Punctuality demanded		.033		.005		-.037		-.029
R² (adjusted)	.054	.142	.069	.144	.093	.146	.114	.165

Source: 1968, 1974, 1981 waves of the Level of Living Survey, Swedish Institute for Social Research, Stockholm University.

Notes: Respondents are included in the first cohort if they either had a preschooler in 1968 or became a parent by 1974. Similarly respondents in the 1974–81 cohort either had a preschooler in 1974 or became a parent by 1981. For fathers, omitted category is "wife not employed"; for mothers, it is "spouse full time."

[a]Guttman scale of reported fatigue over last two weeks.

[b]Guttman scale of reported symptoms of psychological distress over past year.

[c]t1 represents 1968 for 1968–74 cohort and 1974 for 1974–81 cohort; t2 represents 1974 for the 1968–74 cohort and 1981 for the 1974–81 cohort.

+p < .10; *p < .05; **p < .01.

then increased hours could logically be expected to exacerbate role conflict and overload. Overtime work (more than 40 hours per week) in particular, by oneself or one's spouse, could be stressful in that it necessarily takes time away from parenting and home life. The multivariate models do not show that working overtime affects the worker's own distress or fatigue in any major way. However, having a husband who puts in more than 40 hours per week is positively related to increased psychological distress for employed mothers both in 1974 and in 1981.

These regression equations also point to shift work as an important contributor to the fatigue of mothers but not of fathers in both 1974 and 1981 (see Table 5.4). Women working standard daytime schedules are less likely to experience fatigue in 1974 and 1981.

It is interesting to note the effects on personal well-being of a spouse's working hours as well as the absence of effects of working hours on the well-being of fathers. In fact, the major impact of working hours seems to be its effect on the fatigue experienced by mothers; fathers are not appreciably affected. This finding again underscores the fact that it is mothers who primarily bear the dual burden of work and family obligations. That men whose wives work part time experience less strain only reinforces the picture of a traditional division of labor.

The finding that part-time employment has salutary effects on the well-being of working mothers invites within-group comparisons over the three survey periods. Was there an increase in the well-being of part-time workers from 1968 to 1981? What about potential changes in the well-being of those on parental leave, or of those working full time? Subsequent time-series analyses of the fatigue and psychological strain of individuals making the transition to parenthood just prior to the 1968, 1974, and 1981 surveys revealed no interaction effects between being on leave and year (Moen and Forest, 1989): the beneficial effects of parental leaves were the same in 1974 as in 1981. What did change were the numbers of women taking them. There was, however, a shift in the effect of part-time employment on psychological strain. In 1974, women working less than 35 hours a week were less likely to report psychological strain. But, after controlling for autonomy on the job and leaves of absence, part-time and full-time women workers showed no difference, by 1981, in the likelihood of psychological strain.

The Effects of the Work Environment

We expect that the group with high [work] loads and few resources for control is most exposed from the viewpoint of health, while the converse applies to the group with many resources and low loads. (Gardell et al., 1982, p. 20)

Chapter 4 specified workplace conditions, in addition to working hours, that may promote or impair emotional well-being. Jobs that are described as hectic or monotonous or those requiring a great deal of physical exertion might well affect psychological distress and fatigue.

At a general descriptive level, a number of job characteristics seem related to parents' psychological well-being, although these relationships differ by gender. Mothers and fathers not only experience different workplace conditions but they also react differently to similar conditions. For example, performing monotonous work is positively related to psychological strain for women but not for men in the 1981 sample (see Table 5.5). However, jobs that leave parents feeling mentally or physically exhausted at the end of the work day are significantly related to psychological strain for both fathers and mothers. "Feeling exhausted" describes the subjective reactions of workers to their job situations; it is not surprising that those who perceive themselves as exhausted would evidence other negative symptoms.

Table 5.5. The relationship between conditions in the work environment and the well-being of employed Swedish parents, 1981

Work environment	Fathers (% reporting)[a]		Mothers (% reporting)	
	Psych. strain	Daily fatigue	Psych. strain	Daily fatigue
Physical pressures				
Heavy, manual labor	19.4	42.3**	31.7**	46.2
Not demanding	13.1	27.1**	18.1	36.3
Physically exhausting	25.6**	53.7**	43.2**	63.7**
Not exhausting	13.1**	28.1**	18.9**	33.7**
Psychological pressures				
Mentally strenuous	19.3+	37.4	28.1	44.9+
Not strenuous	12.5	29.9	21.6	37.1+
Hectic	15.9	32.7	22.7	39.6
Not hectic	17.0	33.4	27.3	43.0
Monotonous	19.5	45.8*	28.8**	62.1***
Not monotonous	15.1	31.6*	21.3**	35.8***
Work mentally exhausting	29.6***	32.2+	52.9***	65.3***
Not exhausting	12.1***	21.4+	29.2***	33.6***
Autonomy				
Can leave easily for 30 min.	12.6*	36.8*	23.5	35.8*
Can't leave without notifying supervisor	21.8*	30.4*	26.8	41.9*

Source: 1981 wave of the Level of Living Survey, Swedish Institute for Social Research, Stockholm University.

[a]$N = 446$ for fathers, 390 for mothers.

$+p < .10$; $*p < .05$; $**p < .01$; $***p < .001$.

As one would expect, the physical demands of the job are directly related to fatigue. Physically strenuous, dirty, or noisy work is positively related to fatigue. Physical or mental exhaustion at the end of the work day is related to daily tiredness, as it was to psychological distress. Mentally strenuous work, however, is not correlated with feelings of physical fatigue.

Another key attribute of employment is the amount of discretion or the degree of autonomy a worker exercises on the job. One would expect autonomy to be positively related to well-being, insofar as decision-making latitude on the job has been shown to have a direct relationship to psychological functioning in studies of both U.S. and Swedish workers (Karasek, 1979, 1981; Kohn, 1980; Miller et al., 1979; Gardell et al., 1982; Kohn and Schooler, 1983; Mortimer and Lorence, 1979; Gardell and Johansson, 1981). One important form of this autonomy for working parents is their ability to leave work for, say, half an hour without having to report to a superior. And this prerogative is, in fact, associated with fewer symptoms of psychological distress for fathers (although not for mothers). Moreover, parents experiencing this kind of discretion on the job are less likely than those in more controlled work situations to report feelings of daily fatigue (see Table 5.5). This kind of autonomy may well be indicative of a still broader decision-making latitude on the job that influences well-being.

Multivariate Analysis

The direct effects of various features of the work environment on the two measures of well-being, with controls for other factors, are illustrated in Table 5.4. Included in the regression equations are direct and lagged (over the previous six years) measures of the job's physical and psychological pressures. The goals here are to determine: (1) whether job conditions affect well-being once other family and individual factors are taken into account, and (2) whether it is previous, persistent, or current conditions that most account for changes in mental health. Psychological pressures include whether the job is depicted as either mentally strenuous or monotonous, and physical pressures include different physical demands such as having to lift heavy weights. The results show that the current psychological demands of the job are the most important in estimating the well-being of mothers and fathers in both the 1968–74 and 1974–81 cohorts. Fatigue and strain are each influenced by work-related psychological pressures. More detailed analyses reveal that jobs which are viewed as psychologically taxing and those that are monotonous both promote fatigue and psychological distress.

The obverse side of job pressures is the degree of self-direction permitted. The two chief executive officers I interviewed in 1983 stressed the satisfaction growing out of "being the ultimate decision-maker" and "having the power to influence the direction of the company." But for most of the working parents I interviewed, self-direction was discussed in more limited terms, such as their ability to "plan time" and make "flexible arrangements." To test for these possible salutary effects, the various measures of self-direction employed in the Level of Living Survey—the ability to take half an hour off, the required use of a time-clock, and the ability to set one's own pace on the job—were included in the multivariate estimations. However, after controlling for working hours and job pressures, none of these variables had a statistically significant effect in alleviating either fatigue or psychological distress. Moen and Forest (1989) in a more extensive analysis of first-time parents in the Level of Living Survey, found that autonomy—the ability easily to leave the job for a short period—reduced the likelihood of mothers' psychological strain, fatigue, and physical exhaustion as well as the mental exhaustion of fathers. However, that analysis did not control for previous levels of well-being or the nature of the work environment itself.

It may be that autonomy interacts with other job factors to promote well-being. For example, workplace discretion may be particularly valuable in jobs that are marked by high levels of psychological and physical pressure. To assess the impact of job demands in relation to the possible moderating effects of workplace autonomy, log linear models examining the likelihood of strain and fatigue in 1981 were estimated. One variable, the right to leave for a half an hour without supervisory approval, was used as a rough proxy for autonomy on the job.

Neither such autonomy nor job demands (physical and psychological pressures combined) significantly affect the likelihood of fatigue among mothers. However, both affect the probability of fatigue among fathers. In fact, a combination of five factors best predicts the likelihood that fathers will experience daily fatigue: previous (1974) fatigue, wife's employment, family stage, autonomy, and job demands. As would be expected, autonomy and job demands have opposite effects on fatigue, with autonomy somewhat lessening the adverse impacts of employment pressures.

The separate and combined effects of job demands and autonomy are presented in Figure 5.4. It turns out that, controlling for wife's employment, life cycle stage, and previous fatigue, there is an interaction between autonomy and job demands in estimating the likelihood of fatigue for fathers in the 1974–81 cohort (see Figure 5.4). There is little difference in the likelihood of fatigue between fathers whose jobs entail little pressure and those who only recently moved into jobs making con-

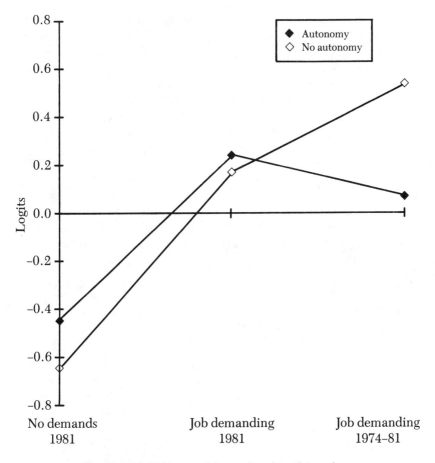

Effect parameters (lambdas) of logit model controlling for wife's employment, previous fatigue, and family stage

Model is FWX FDA FS SDWAX ($G^2 = 71.80$, d.f. $= 54$, $p = .053$, $N = 644$)

Figure 5.4. Likelihood of Swedish fathers experiencing fatigue, 1981, by work demands and job autonomy. A = job autonomy, D = job demands, F = daily fatigue (no, yes), S = family stage (new fathers, preschoolers both years, middle childhood), W = employment (working, not working), X = previous fatigue (no, yes).

Source: 1974, 1981 waves of the Level of Living Survey, Swedish Institute for Social Research, Stockholm University.

siderable demands. However, for those fathers whose jobs were demanding in both 1974 and 1981, autonomy plays an important role in mitigating the negative effects of job pressure on fatigue.[2]

Despite its effects on fatigue, autonomy does not contribute to the estimation of psychological distress for parents once other factors are taken
into account. What does matter are the demands of the job. The effects of
these demands, both psychological and physical, on the likelihood of psychological distress are illustrated in Figure 5.5. It is quite evident once
again that previous (1974) feelings of psychological distress are important.
Those reporting strain in 1974 are likely to continue to do so in 1981. But
also apparent is the effect of job demands. Persistent demands (i.e., in both
1974 and 1981) are most likely to result in psychological strains. For
women, these effects are especially pronounced. Mothers who do not experience job demands are the least likely to report distress, and those mothers
experiencing persistent job demands are the most likely to report it.

The Effects of Employment Insecurity

Crises do not reside within the individual or the situation but
rather arise from interaction between an individual and a particular situation. (Elder, 1974, p. 10)

Much has been written about the deleterious effects on individual well-
being of employment insecurity, be it in the form of actual or expected
job loss. Yet in these Swedish data, being or expecting to be unemployed is
not related to well-being.

When job loss or job impermanence are included in a multivariate
model, I find that, on the whole, the effects of these measures of job insecurity on parental well-being are singularly unimpressive, after controlling for individual, family, and occupational characteristics. This
suggests that government efforts to lessen the incidence, duration, and
economic costs of unemployment have been successful in mitigating their
emotional costs as well. Moreover, being on a job described as "temporary" does not seem to have deleterious effects on parental well-being.

These findings deviate sharply from what is known about unemployment and job insecurity in the United States (see, for example, Bronfenbrenner and Crouter, 1982; Kahn, 1981; Moen, 1983; Moen et al.,

2. Autonomy, measured in terms of the ability to leave the job for brief periods, could
well be reflective of a more wide-ranging freedom from supervision and latitude for decision that have been shown to have positive impacts on self-concept and well-being,
especially among men. See Kohn and Schooler, 1983; Karasek, 1979, 1981; Miller et al.,
1979.

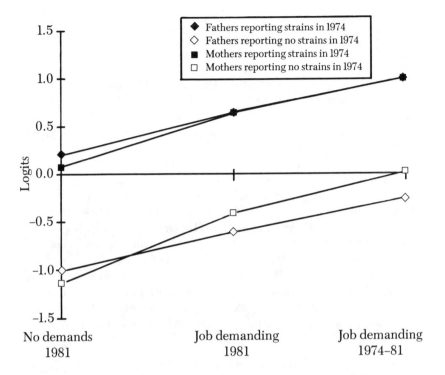

For men: Effect parameters (lambdas) of logit model controlling for family stage
Model is PSO PD SDAWO (G^2 = 51.85, d.f. = 55, p = .59, N = 644 [fathers])
For women: Effect parameters (lambdas) of logit model
Model is PD PO DAOHS (G^2 = 78.64, d.f. = 55, p = 15, N = 589 [mothers])

Figure 5.5. Likelihood of psychological strain of employed Swedish parents, 1981, by job demands and previous strain. A = job autonomy, D = job demands, O = previous strains (no, yes), P = psychological strain (no, yes), S = family stage (new fathers, preschoolers both years, middle childhood), W = wife employed (no, yes), H = work hours.

Source: 1974, 1981 waves of the Level of Living Survey, Swedish Institute for Social Research, Stockholm University.

1984). Here the emotional distress of the threat or the reality of joblessness may well reflect the social and economic costs borne by the unemployed. This is in contrast to Sweden, a nation explicitly committed to full employment and economic security.

The Physical and Mental Exhaustion of Working Parents

The researcher looks only at the social address—that is, an environmental label, with no systematic examination of what the environment is like, what people are living there, what they are doing, or how the activities taking place could affect the child. (Bronfenbrenner, 1982, pp. 7–8)

Reports of psychological distress and daily fatigue are strongly related to feelings of both physical and mental exhaustion at the end of the work day for mothers and fathers alike (see Table 5.6). Adding these two measures of exhaustion to the regression equations accounts for substantially more variance in explaining parental fatigue and psychological distress. But what, in turn, accounts for these feelings of work-related exhaustion in parents? Looking at the 1974–81 cohort, 23 percent of employed mothers and 17 percent of fathers reported in 1981 that they felt physically exhausted after work, virtually the same proportions as were found in the 1968–74 cohort. Only slightly smaller proportions of the 1974–81 cohort, 20 percent of mothers and 16 percent of fathers, reported feelings of mental exhaustion at the end of the working day, again not significantly different from the finding for the 1968–74 cohort.

One may assume that job conditions, rather than family factors, would be most likely to explain the physical and mental exhaustion of fathers, whereas a combination of work and family factors would explain the exhaustion of employed mothers. Again this is because the family "work"

Table 5.6. Effects of physical and mental exhaustion[a] after work on changes in measures of well-being of employed Swedish parents (metric coefficients)

	Fathers	Mothers
Effects of physical exhaustion		
1968–74 cohort		
Fatigue	.211***	.192***
Psychological strain	.132***	.078***
1974–81 cohort:		
Fatigue	.165***	.117*
Psychological strain	.088*	.154***
Effects of psychological exhaustion		
1968–74 cohort		
Fatigue	.129**	.113*
Psychological strain	.125**	.150**
1974–81 cohort		
Fatigue	.169***	.164***
Psychological strain	.075+	.023

Source: 1968, 1974, 1981 waves of the Level of Living Survey, Swedish Institute for Social Research, Stockholm University.

N: (1968–74 cohort) men = 678, women = 487; (1974–81 cohort) men = 676, women = 575.

[a]Includes background variables and previous well-being as well as occupational factors.
+$p < .10$; *$p < .05$; **$p < .01$; ***$p < .001$.

of tending (as well as attending) to home and children can itself be exhausting and it is a responsibility that falls disproportionately on the wife and mother.

The data do indeed suggest that fathers are exhausted principally by their experience on the job. But they also suggest that this is true for working mothers. For both parents, work conditions contribute to the estimation of both physical and mental exhaustion. Most influential in determining the fatigue of parents are the physical demands of their jobs. Those engaged in manual labor, for instance, requiring the lifting of heavy objects, are predictably exhausted at the end of the day. But a monotonous job or one that is described as "hectic" also contributes to physical exhaustion (see Table 5.7).

Mental exhaustion, in contrast, is related to the performance of tasks that are psychologically taxing and hectic, not physically demanding. Moreover, it is only in estimating the physical and mental exhaustion of fathers that we see life stage exerting any direct effects. In both the

Table 5.7. Likelihood of physical and mental exhaustion of the end of the working day for employed Swedish parents (metric coefficients)

| | Fathers | | | | Mothers | | | |
| | Physical exhaustion | | Mental exhaustion | | Physical exhaustion | | Mental exhaustion | |
	1974	1981	1974	1981	1974	1981	1974	1981
(N)	(678)	(676)	(678)	(676)	(487)	(575)	(487)	(575)
Physical pressures of job								
t1	.088*	.079+	.007	.026	.083+	.072	.031	−.045
t2	.199***	.218***	.000	.027	.346***	.376***	.000	.038
Psychological pressures of job								
Hectic	.065	.173**	.080*	.071	.123**	.035	.042	.023
Monotonous	.092*	.098*	.020	.023	.170***	.043	.090*	.023
Psychologically taxing	.052	.041	.346***	.336***	.072	.035	.451***	.440***
Upper	−.043	.078	.042	.102*	−.145*	.052	.042	−.115*
Working	−.017	.091+	−.016	.026	.111*	.106*	.035	.030
Overtime	−.002	.047	−.003	.092*	.017	.013	.006	−.054
Leave last week	−.024	−.021	−.007	−.023	−.016	−.017	−.011	.086*
Leave last year	.037	−.011	.015	−.073	−.021	.036	.042	.011
R^2 (adjusted)	.114	.189	.189	.166	.280	.241	.228	.251

Source: 1968, 1974, 1981 waves of the Level of Living Survey, Swedish Institute for Social Research, Stockholm University.

$+p < .10$; $*p < .05$; $**p < .01$; $***p < .001$.

1968–74 and 1974–81 cohorts, fathers with children moving into the school-age years are more likely than those with preschoolers still in the home to report both physical and mental exhaustion. There are a number of possible explanations. Fathers may increase their investment in their jobs as they (and their children) grow older. Or, as children grow older, the involvement of the father may change. However, research underscores the limited involvement of fathers with their children at all stages of parenting (Coverman and Sheley, 1986; Haas, 1982; Miller and Garrison, 1982).

Quality of Life

How do conditions at work affect parents' assessments of their life situations generally? Controlling for background factors, the working conditions that seem to matter most for employed mothers have to do with the scheduling and number of working hours (see Table 5.8). Women who are on leave, who are working part time, and who are able easily to leave work for brief periods are more likely to positively evaluate the quality of their lives. Working nonstandard shifts contributes to a more negative evaluation. The toll that work time and scheduling exact from working mothers includes not only their feelings of well-being and work-related exhaustion but also their overall appraisal of their life conditions.

Wives whose husbands work more than 40 hours a week are also more positive, possibly reflecting their satisfaction with spouses who are fulfilling the traditional breadwinner role. Note that this conflicts with the findings on women's psychological strain, which is higher for those whose husbands put in long hours on the job. But this points to the difference between cognitive satisfaction with the quality of one's life and emotional distress. Wives whose husbands are in working–class jobs are typically less positive about the condition of their lives, regardless of their own occupational status.

Husbands whose wives work part time are more likely to positively assess the quality of their lives, while those with wives working more than 40 hours a week are less satisfied. Men in working–class occupations also are generally less satisfied, as are those whose jobs impose psychological pressures.

This measure of general life satisfaction approaches well-being from a different and much broader perspective than that provided by reports of psychological distress or fatigue, but the picture it paints conforms to the ones presented earlier in this chapter. For mothers what matters most is working hours. For fathers what matters most is their spouses' working

Table 5.8. Assessment of conditions of living, 1974–81 cohort (metric coefficients)

	Fathers	Mothers
(N)	(676)	(575)
Working hours and scheduling		
Part-time	.012	-.086+
Overtime	-.011	-.064
Shift work	.050	.074+
Leave last week	.031	-.095*
Leave last year	.015	.007
Spouse full-time	-.085*	—
Spouse part-time	-.120**	.068
Spouse overtime	.064+	-.114**
Working environment		
Physical pressures,		
t1	.034	-.074
t2	-.019	-.031
Psychological pressures,		
t1	-.011	.030
t2	.065+	-.006
Occupational level		
Upper	.023	-.040
Working	.098+	.082
Spouse–upper	—	-.021
Spouse–working class	—	.144***
Self-direction		
Autonomy	-.055	-.122**
Sets own pace	-.013	.024
Punctuality demanded	.026	.032
R^2 (adjusted)	.139	.168

Source: 1974, 1981 waves of the Level of Living Survey, Swedish Institute for Social Research, Stockholm University.
— = not included in equation.
$+p < .10$; $*p < .05$; $**p < .01$; $***p < .001$.
Note: Positive coefficient means a negative appraisal.

hours. Thus, the time and timing of work, along with location in the social structure, affect not only parents' emotional distress but also the quality of their lives.

Working Conditions and Well-Being: Sweden and the United States

The findings reported in this chapter emphasize the importance of the work environment—above and beyond labor force status—for parental well-being. Even after controlling for background factors, such as family characteristics and previous levels of well-being, we find that psychological and physical job pressures influence the psychological strains and fatigue levels experienced by working parents. But we also see gender differences in the way various working conditions affect well-being; working hours, for instance, are related to women's fatigue but not to men's.

Some suggest that the differential well-being of workers in various jobs is a result of occupational *selection*—certain types of individuals seek out certain jobs. Others posit a process of occupational *socialization*, wherein job conditions affect the individuals occupying them (see discussions by Kohn and Schooler, 1983; Mortimer et al., 1986). In this study, I control for previous levels of well-being and in that way attempt to control for selection. Thus these findings also reveal the complexity of this process, suggesting that the characteristics parents bring *to* the job, by way of previous well-being as well as gender-related family responsibilities, moderate the effects of the characteristics *of* the job on their emotional health.

Whether because of legislated changes in employment conditions and benefits, changes in the social attitudes supporting maternal employment, or both, combining employment with the raising of preschoolers in Sweden became less stressful for women in 1981 than it was in 1968. Moreover, one legislated benefit, the option of reducing one's working hours to a part-time schedule while children are preschoolers, appears to have beneficial effects on working mothers, reducing the likelihood of distress and fatigue, lessening feelings of work-related exhaustion, and increasing general satisfaction with one's conditions of life. For men, having a wife working part time also appears to have positive effects on emotional health and life satisfaction.

Conversely, jobs making major physical and psychological demands exacerbate the distress, fatigue, and exhaustion of mothers as well as fathers. But some discretion on the job, as evidenced in the ability to leave work for a brief period, is positively associated with well-being, especially for fathers, and reduces the deleterious effects of persistent job demands on fathers' fatigue.

There are, to be sure, gender differences in both the conditions of work and the effects of these conditions on well-being. But controlling for previous distress virtually eliminates differences by gender in the effects of job demands on psychological strain. Mothers and fathers who reported high distress in 1974 and whose jobs are demanding also have the same high probability of distress in 1981.

It could be argued that the salutary aspects of part-time schedules are bought at a price—that part-time workers have different kinds of jobs and, hence, poorer conditions of employment. But this possibility is unlikely for this age group, since a considerable proportion are simply reducing the hours of their regular full-time jobs while their children are young. Moreover, an analysis of psychological and physical job demands in relation to time worked reveals no significant difference in the pressures experienced on the job by part- and full-time workers.

Unfortunately, no comparable body of data is available to assess the well-being of working parents of young children in the United States. The best existing data source, the U.S. Department of Labor's Quality of Employment Survey (QES), is limited in that it sampled only workers who put in 20 or more hours a week on the job and was last conducted in 1977. But a recent analysis of the QES data for parents of young children (Willer, 1986) does suggest many similarities in the effects of working conditions on parental well-being.

One measure included in the Quality of Employment Survey assesses "work–family interference" by asking the question, "How much do your job and your family life interfere with each other?" Variables related to the scheduling of work seem to contribute most to an explanation of work-family interference for employed parents, both fathers and mothers, in the United States. In multivariate analyses, the number of hours spent on the job and shift work were both strongly related to the experience of work–family conflicts. And the ability to take time off for personal reasons reduced the likelihood of such conflicts.

Two other variables included in the Quality of Employment Survey bear some resemblance to the questions on well-being addressed in the Swedish study. One is a self-reported evaluation of health and the other an evaluation of energy level. Time spent on the job is negatively related to feelings of energy for working parents in the United States, as it was for employed Swedish mothers. And the mothers and fathers in the United States who can take time off the job for personal matters are the ones most likely to report high levels of health. But in the United States, as in Sweden, it is working mothers, not fathers, who are most likely to report low levels of energy, even though it is the fathers who typically put in more hours on the job (Moen and Moorehouse, 1983; Moen and Dempster-McClain, 1987; Willer, 1986).

Thus, in the United States, as in Sweden, workplace experiences "spill over" into the home by affecting the well-being of working parents. But we do not yet know the long-term consequences of this spillover, nor have we established the moderating effects of one variable upon another, as with workplace autonomy and initial level of parental well-being in the case of Swedish parents.

The findings reported in this chapter, as well as in studies of working parents in the United States, suggest comparable conclusions regarding the effects of job pressures, working hours, and work schedules. (Piotrkowski, 1979. Piotrkowski and Crits-Cristoph, 1981; Staines and

Pleck, 1983; Pleck and Staines, 1985; Willer, 1986; Wethington, 1987).
Future research can no longer look only at the effects of employment per
se on well-being but must take into account family conditions and the
specific nature of the work environment. And a particularly important
component of that environment appears to be flexibility—for mothers,
being able to reduce their working hours, for fathers, being able to leave
the job for short periods of time. This research also supports the conclusion that employment conditions do indeed touch the lives of children
directly, by requiring parents to be absent from the home, but also indirectly, by affecting parents' emotional health and energy level.

6

Parental Well-Being in Context

Chapters 3 and 5 dealt with continuity and change in parental well-being in broad terms. This chapter presents a more finely tuned analysis. Thus far I have reported that psychological distress and fatigue are differently experienced by working men and women in Sweden, but that these gender differences decreased from the late 1960s to the early 1980s. I have also linked differences in distress and fatigue to location in the social structure, as defined by occupational status. Mothers in working-class jobs are the most likely to express feelings of fatigue and symptoms of psychological strain. Working-class fathers are disproportionately prone to fatigue, but men in professional and managerial positions are the most likely to report psychological distress. And we have seen that various employment conditions account for changes, from one survey to the next, in the well-being of individual men and women in two cohorts, 1968–74 and 1974–81. Working hours emerged as an especially important factor in reducing the strains and fatigue of employed mothers.

This chapter examines changes in the well-being of particular *sub-groups* of working parents in Sweden. Individuals who are both workers and parents can be found at different levels in the occupational hierarchy and in different situations, both at home and at work. The first part of the chapter divides the sample into two broad groupings: white-collar employees (professionals, managers, technicians, clerical) and working-

115

class, blue-collar employees. Do the same factors influence well-being for each of these groups?

The second part extends earlier discussions of well-being by life-cycle stage (Chapter 3) by examining individuals who became parents between surveys. What factors affect the well-being of men and women making the important transition to parenthood?

Finally, because initial level of well-being has proved to be the single most important factor in estimating subsequent levels of strain and fatigue, the third part of this chapter focuses on two additional subgroups, defined on the basis of their reports of strain and fatigue. Here I examine two groups of women who first became mothers between 1968 and 1974 or 1974 and 1981: those who experienced *both* strain and fatigue during the survey period prior to childbirth and those who reported neither strain nor fatigue prior to childbirth.

My aim is to introduce into the analysis the contextual realities that working parents bring to the job. Work life is not separate and distinct from the rest of one's life, and moving into parenthood may alter the effects of the work environment on well-being. Women who previously experienced a great deal of stress may find that conditions on the job only heighten their difficulties. Moreover, we must attend to contextual factors in the work environment itself. Chapter 4 showed how markedly job conditions vary by location in the occupational hierarchy. But what about people in very different kinds of jobs who have similar working conditions? Do the *same* conditions differentially affect well-being for parents in white-collar and blue-collar jobs?

Differences by Social Class

Members of different social classes by virtue of enjoying (or suffering) different conditions of life come to see the world differently—to develop different conceptions of reality, different aspirations and hopes and fears, different conceptions of the desirable. (Kohn, 1977, p. 7)

The data presented thus far on Swedish parents corroborate Kohn's observation about the significance of location in the social structure for individual well-being. One way of explaining these class differences is in terms of the differential distribution of deleterious working conditions, as described in Chapter 4. Members of the working class may report greater fatigue because the jobs they perform are in fact more physically gruelling. And men in upper-level occupations may report more symptoms of distress because their work is more psychologically demanding than that typically done by men in lower-echelon jobs.

But there could be still another explanation. To be sure, white-collar workers differ from blue-collar workers in their working conditions. But they also differ, as Kohn suggests, in the way they perceive and define their world. Being in a white-collar job may lessen or, conversely, exacerbate the otherwise deleterious effects of the work environment. A professional may regard a job with considerable time pressure as challenging and stimulating, whereas the service worker may view similar pressures as excessive and burdensome. Professionals may see psychological pressures as voluntary and self-imposed, and hence desirable, whereas those lower on the occupational ladder may react to these pressures as an unwelcome demand imposed by supervisors.

Multivariate Analysis

What do the Level of Living Survey data reveal about class differences among Swedish parents? I estimated multivariate models that include controls for individual and family factors separately, for working and middle/upper-class parents.[1] The results suggest similarities as well as differences among them (see Table 6.1). In the case of fatigue, both mothers and fathers at all occupational levels are adversely affected by the psychological pressures they experience on the job. Moreover, except for working-class mothers in the 1974–81 cohort, it appears to be *current* job pressures, rather than those experienced during the previous survey period, that lead to fatigue. Working irregular hours (shifts) is also related to fatigue, but only for mothers in working-class jobs—and over one in three mothers in blue-collar jobs works shifts, compared to one in ten in white-collar (middle and upper level) jobs. Furthermore, the working-class mothers in the 1974–81 cohort seem to benefit most from part-time employment: they have a lower likelihood of fatigue. In contrast, the detrimental effects of long hours on the job are most apparent for women in white-collar jobs; these women are more prone to fatigue if they work more than a 40-hour week.

Psychological pressures on the job also contribute to psychological distress among Swedish fathers, regardless of their location in the occupational hierarchy, but affect only mothers in working-class jobs. Interestingly, it is working-class fathers who benefit most, as shown in lower levels of psychological distress, from having wives who work less than full time.

Fathers in white-collar occupations present quite a puzzle. Very little

1. Because professionals have very different kinds of jobs, with different demands, pay scales, socializations, I also included "upper class" as a dummy variable in the multivariate analyses.

Table 6.1. Factors affecting various measures of well-being, by social class and gender, 1974–81 cohort of employed parents

A. Fathers

	White-collar					Blue-collar				
	Psychological distress	Daily fatigue	Quality of life	Physical exhaustion	Psychological exhaustion	Psychological distress	Daily fatigue	Quality of life	Physical exhaustion	Psychological exhaustion
Individual and family characteristics										
Age		+	+			+				
Education		+	+			+				
Physical limitations		+	+							
Residence										
Metropolitan		+								
Rural							−	−		
Family size						−				
Life stage										
New parent, 1981					+					
Middle childhood, 1981				+						
Working hours and scheduling										
Part-time										
Overtime					+					+
Shift work					−					+
Leave last week	+									
Leave last year										
Spouse part-time						−		−		
Spouse overtime										
Working environment										
Physical pressures, t1				+					+	
Physical pressures, t2									+	
Psychological pressures, t1						−				
Psychological pressures, t2	+				+	+	+		+	+
Occupational level										
Upper	+									
Spouse-working										
Self-direction										
Autonomy										
Sets own pace										
R^2	.034	.097	.100	.206	.220	.284	.185	.069	.119	.165

118

B. Mothers

Individual and family characteristics										
Age		−				−		−		
Education										
Physical limitations				+		+	+	+		
Residence										
Metropolitan			+					+		
Rural			+							
Family size		+								
Marital status		+			+	+	+	+		
Single parent										
Life stage										
New parent, 1981							−			
Middle childhood, 1981										
Working hours and scheduling										
Part-time		+				+		−		
Overtime		+					+	+		
Shift work		+					−	+		
Leave last week					+					
Leave last year										−
Spouse part-time		−								
Spouse overtime							+			−
Working environment										
Physical pressures, t1				+	+					
Physical pressures, t2				+	+		+		+	
Psychological pressures, t1							+	+		
Psychological pressures, t2					+	+	+			+
Occupational level										
Upper	−				−	−				
Spouse-working			+							
Self-direction										
Autonomy										
Sets own pace										
R^2	.119	.132	.182	.236	.201	.181	.236	.108	.143	.274

Source: 1974, 1981 waves of the Level of Living Survey, Swedish Institute for Social Research, Stockholm University.
Note: + (−) = Factors statistically significant in contributing to higher (lower) levels of psychological distress, daily fatigue, and physical/psychological exhaustion at end of working day, and lower (higher) appraisal of quality of life. t1 = 1974; t2 = 1981. For fathers, N = 381 (white-collar), 295 (blue-collar); for mothers, N = 313 (white-collar), 262 (blue-collar).

of the variance ($R^2 = .034$) in psychological distress among middle- and upper-level fathers can be explained by any of the family, individual, or occupational characteristics included in these estimations. In fact, once I controlled for psychological pressures and previous well-being, the only variable that proved to have statistical significance was whether the father held a professional or managerial job. We have seen that these men in upper-level occupations are more prone to psychological distress than are any other group; this remains true even after controlling for a good many other occupational and personal characteristics. Clearly the factors producing the psychological distress of fathers in white-collar jobs—particularly those in professional or managerial occupations—have not been captured in the variables included in this analysis.

Working-class fathers present another picture. Over one-fourth of the variance ($R^2 = 4.284$) in their reports of distress in 1981 can be explained: age, psychological pressures, and health problems all increase the likelihood of distress, and family size, a wife working part time, and a manual job (one imposing physical demands) reduce the probability of distress among male blue-collar workers. Manual jobs per se typically do not tax the worker's mental or emotional resources, although they may require considerable physical exertion.

Although women in working-class occupations are more likely to report psychological distress than are those in middle- and upper-level jobs, their current distress is contingent on previous levels of strain. Log linear analysis reveals an interaction: those women who reported strains in 1974 were the most vulnerable to psychological distress in 1981, those who reported no psychological distress in 1974 were the least prone to distress in 1981 (see Figure 6.1). Apparently, being in a working-class job can exacerbate the psychological difficulties of women, but only for those already prone to such difficulties.

Quality of Life

One the whole, survey respondents were quite positive in rating their general life situation. But do parents at different levels in the occupational hierarchy evaluate the conditions of their lives similarly, or do these assessments vary as a function of social class?

Multivariate analysis reveals that for mothers in working-class jobs, working part time, overtime, or being on a leave of absence contribute to more positive feelings about their quality of life.[2] Working overtime contributes to women's fatigue, but it also contributes additional income.

2. This survey question is coded on a 1–5 scale: the higher the score, the worse the evaluation.

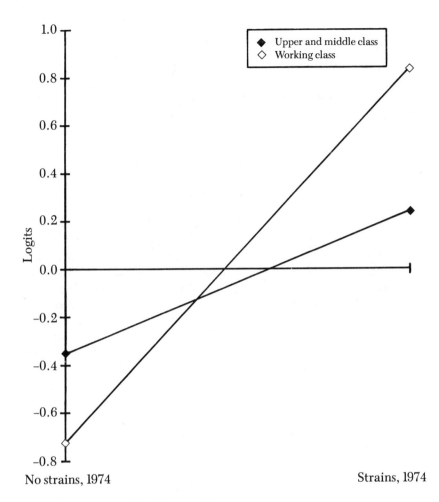

No strains, 1974   Strains, 1974

Effect parameters (lambdas) of logit model
Model is PD PF PSO PEC ESCFDO (G^2 = 56.8, d.f. = 60, p = .059)

Figure 6.1. Likelihood of employed Swedish mothers experiencing psychological strain,
by social class and previous strain. In logit model, P = psychological strain, 1981,
E = employment 1974, S = social class, C = living conditions, F = physical demands
of work, D = psychological demands of work, O = psychological strain, 1974.

   Source: 1974, 1981 waves of the Level of Living Survey, Swedish Institute for Social
Research, Stockholm University.

Women choosing to work longer hours may therefore see this as directly enhancing their family's standard of living and quality of life. Single-parent status and shift work both foster less positive evaluations (see Table 6.1).

For mothers with white-collar jobs, being a single parent or having a spouse in a blue-collar occupation both contribute to a more negative evaluation of the quality of life. Conversely, having a husband who puts in more than 40 hours a week contributes to a positive assessment of life conditions by these women. Again, this may reflect wives' judgments of their husbands' fulfillment of the breadwinner role—the "good provider" may well be one who puts in more than the standard 40-hour week.

What about the quality of life of Swedish fathers? Those in white-collar occupations are more positive about the conditions of their lives if they have at least some college education, and are more negative with advancing age. Fathers in blue-collar jobs assess their life conditions more positively if their wives are working part time and if they live in rural areas.

The Level of Living Survey also questioned respondents about changes in life conditions, asking whether their lives were getting better or worse. The responses of fathers, but not mothers, were related to their social class. More than a fourth (26.7 percent) of the fathers in working-class jobs depicted their lives as having gotten worse over the last five years, whereas fewer than a sixth (13 percent) of those in higher-level occupations felt their living conditions had worsened.

Social Class and Well-Being: Conclusions

Class differences in well-being are related to differences in the employment conditions experienced, but here the picture is more complicated. Some conditions, such as psychological pressures at work, contribute to the fatigue and distress of both blue- and white-collar workers. The negative effects of psychological pressures on the job do not appear to be affected by the location of the job on the occupational ladder. But other working conditions do have differential effects according to occupational level. For example, part-time employment appears to be especially beneficial for both women in working-class jobs *and* for their spouses (that is, for working-class husbands whose wives are on part-time hours). And men in professional jobs tend to report high levels of psychological distress regardless of the specific conditions of their work.

Which working parents in Sweden are *most* likely to enjoy well-being? Certainly not single-parent mothers, who, regardless of social class, are more prone to symptoms of psychological distress. Certainly not fathers in professional and managerial jobs, nor parents exposed to psychological job pressures; these last are more likely to report both fatigue and distress than others.

The working-class fathers most likely to express a general sense of well-being are relatively young, have large families, live in rural areas of Sweden, and have wives who are employed part time. Middle-class fathers who are also relatively young and healthy and who have advanced levels of education are also better off, both in reduced levels of fatigue and strain and in the general quality of their lives.

Employed mothers most apt to experience well-being are professionals who are somewhat older than others in this life stage and who have small families. Working-class mothers are better off if they too are older with few children, but also if they live in rural areas and have husbands who are not working part time.

Transition to Parenthood

A major turning point during the adult years is, of course, the experience of parenthood.[3] Whether this life transition results in corresponding shifts in well-being is not at all clear. A popular and seemingly perennial sociological issue concerns the psychological effects of the transition to parenthood (LeMasters, 1957; Rossi, 1968, 1984; Entwisle and Doering, 1981; LaRossa and LaRossa, 1981). Studies to date have reported mixed results regarding the effects of becoming a parent on well-being (cf. Lamb, 1978) but none thus far have included in their analyses the characteristics of parents' jobs.

When, as reported in Chapter 5, life-cycle stage was included in the multivariate models, it had no direct effect on well-being independent of other variables. But life-cycle stage may well indirectly influence the effects of working conditions on well-being. Specifically, individuals relatively new to parenthood may be more vulnerable than parents who are experienced in juggling the cross-pressures of work and family. Accordingly, I selected a subsample of childless individuals who became parents between 1974 and 1981. My goal was to look at the child-bearing phase of adulthood not only in relation to family characteristics that might affect well-being, but also with reference to employment conditions. *Both* mothers and fathers are now increasingly in the labor force during this life stage, and it is imperative to identify factors in their employment situations that particularly enhance or impair their well-being.

3. Marriage is also a major life transition in adulthood. But given the widespread acceptance and the prevalence of cohabitation in Sweden and the combined totals for married and cohabiting in the Level of Living Survey, I cannot examine this transition.

Becoming a Parent

The transition to parenthood apparently became easier for employed Swedish mothers from 1968 to 1981 (see Figure 6.2). In 1968, over half of the employed women who had become mothers within the last six years reported fatigue, and over one-third (36.6 percent) experienced symptoms of psychological distress. By 1981, only two-fifths (38.4 percent) were fatigued and a little over a fourth (27.7 percent) distressed. Similar declines are also evident in their reports of both physical and psychological work-related exhaustion. But among men who became fathers there were no comparable decreases—indeed, the proportion experiencing fatigue rose slightly, from 31.4 percent in 1968 to 34.3 percent in 1981. Feelings of mental and physical exhaustion after work also increased

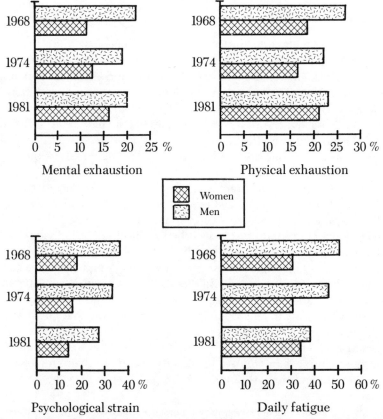

Figure 6.2. Distributions of various measures of well-being: workers making the transition to parenthood within the last six years (*N* = 1445).

Source: 1974, 1981 waves of the Level of Living Survey, Swedish Institute for Social Research, Stockholm University.

among these men from 1968 to 1981. Thus, by 1981, the well-being of those making the transition to parenthood had improved for mothers but declined somewhat for fathers.

First-Time Parents, 1981

In the 1974 survey these respondents were childless; by the 1981 survey they had experienced one or more births and were busy establishing their families. By 1981, 50 percent had one child, 43 percent had two children, and the remaining 7 percent had three children.

Most of these parents described their conditions of life as having recently improved.[4] There were gender differences, however. Fewer men (43 percent) than women (52 percent) depicted their lives as improving; 19 percent of the men and only 14 percent of the women reported that it had worsened during the years when they had become parents.

The average age of the men who had become fathers by 1981 was thirty-two. Nearly half were in blue-collar occupations and only 12 percent held professional or managerial jobs. A fifth were on some kind of nonstandard shift, 7 percent worked more than 40 hours a week, and fewer than 4 percent were on part-time schedules. About a tenth had either been on a leave of absence in the last year or were currently on leave. Over half (56 percent) had wives who worked part time.

Women making the transition to motherhood by 1981 were somewhat younger than men becoming fathers, twenty-nine years on average. About 7 percent were single parents, neither married nor cohabiting. Nine percent had been employed in 1974 but had left the labor force by 1981. Over a fifth had entered the labor force between surveys, and almost two-thirds were employed in both 1974 and 1981. Fewer than 10 percent were not in the labor force either year. Comparatively few (6.4 percent) were in professional jobs; 58.7 percent were in middle-class occupations, and somewhat over a third (34.9 percent) held working-class jobs. Of the mothers in the labor force, over a fourth were on leave of absence in 1981, almost two-fifths had been on leave the preceding year, and three-fifths were working less than full time in 1981.

Fatigue and Psychological Distress

What factors influenced the well-being of individuals who became parents between 1974 and 1981? Multivariate analyses reveal that employment status per se had little effect on the women who became mothers. But living in a large city and having had more than one child between 1974 and 1981 both contributed to increased levels of fatigue (see Table 6.2).

4. The survey question asked about changes in conditions of life over the last five years.

Table 6.2. Factors affecting various measures of well-being for employed first-time parents, 1974–81 cohort

	Fathers (N = 218)					Mothers (N = 139)				
	Psychological distress	Daily fatigue	Quality of life	Physical exhaustion	Psychological exhaustion	Psychological distress	Daily fatigue	Quality of life	Physical exhaustion	Psychological exhaustion
Individual and family characteristics										
Age			+		+		–			–
Education				–						
Physical limitations				–						
Residence										
Metropolitan							+			
Rural							+			
Family size		–					+			
Marital status										
Single parent	–							+		
Working hours and scheduling										
Part-time	+						–	–		
Overtime					+		+			
Leave last week	–									
Spouse part-time								–		
Spouse overtime									–	
Working environment										
Physical pressures, 1981	+			+					+	
Psychological pressures, 1974	+				+					
Psychological pressures, 1981							+			
Occupational level										
Upper	+									
Working			+			–				
Spouse–working							+		+	
Self-direction										
Autonomy	–	–	–			–				
Sets own pace	+	+				+				
R^2	.111	.053	.138	.100	.175	.221	.122	.153	.173	1.59

Source: 1974, 1981 waves of the Level of Living Survey, Swedish Institute for Social Research, Stockholm University.

Note: + (–) = Factors statistically significant in contributing to higher (lower) levels of psychological distress, daily fatigue, physical/psychological exhaustion at end of working day, and lower (higher) appraisal of quality of life.

Among those who were in the labor force in 1981, combining motherhood with employment, older women, surprisingly, reported less fatigue than did their younger counterparts. Not unexpectedly, working more than 40 hours a week led to an increase in fatigue, as did psychological pressures on the job, whereas part-time hours reduced its likelihood.

When we turn again to the other measure of well-being, psychological distress, employment does not appear to account for any changes in women's reports of distress during this life stage. Very probably, then, it is the family situation, rather than workplace conditions, that most influences the psychological distress of first-time mothers.

Only two job-related factors are related to changes in the well-being of men who became fathers by 1981: their freedom to leave the workplace for a half-hour or so and their ability to set the pace of their work. First-time fathers who had the latitude to make decisions about briefly leaving the workplace were likely to report reduced levels of fatigue and distress, but those who could set their own pace of work surprisingly reported *higher* levels of fatigue and symptoms of distress. It may be that those who can determine their own pace are also workers who have or are encouraged to have higher levels of commitment to their jobs. Those few fathers who themselves were working part time in 1981 reported higher levels of psychological distress, but those whose *wives* worked part time reveal reduced levels of distress.

Although professional women who became mothers between 1974 and 1981 experienced a reduced level of strain, the opposite was true of men in professional and managerial jobs who became fathers: they were more likely to report increased distress. We have seen that men with high-status jobs are more vulnerable to psychological distress; apparently this also holds true for those men making the transition to fatherhood. Women in professional occupations who gave birth between 1974 and 1981 also reported less psychological distress than those in working-class or middle-class white-collar jobs.

Quality of Life
Individuals who only recently became parents do not differ significantly from other parents of preschoolers in characterizing the quality of their lives. What most affects these mothers' appraisal of their life conditions is first and foremost marital status: single parents are more likely to be negative. New mothers working part time or on leave of absence, in contrast, are the most likely to be positive. Women whose husbands work part time tend to be more negative, as are those whose spouses are in working-class jobs. And again it is the mothers in professional jobs who are most likely to describe their lives positively.

As with fathers in general, new working-class fathers are more likely to describe their life situation favorably, and older fathers are less likely to be positive than are younger ones. The job characteristic most influencing assessments of the life conditions of fathers is a measure of workplace autonomy.

Physical and Psychological Exhaustion after Work

The picture painted of the physical and psychological work-related exhaustion of individuals who became parents between 1974 and 1981 is similar to that seen for all parents (Chapter 5). About 10 percent of these fathers and 17 percent of the employed mothers reported that they were physically exhausted at the end of the work day. Multivariate analyses reveal that this condition is particularly characteristic of those performing manual jobs. But physical demands aside, women in working-class jobs are still more likely than those in white-collar or professional occupations to report work-related exhaustion, and men with a college education are typically less likely than those with fewer years of education to report such exhaustion.

Slightly more fathers (18 percent) than employed mothers (16 percent) say that they are psychologically exhausted after work; these feelings are related, for both parents, to jobs described as mentally taxing. Older men are more apt to be psychologically exhausted, as are those working more than a 40-hour week. And again, professional women are less likely to report psychological exhaustion than are those in nonprofessional jobs. Working part time decreases the likelihood of psychological exhaustion among first-time mothers but *increases* its likelihood among first-time fathers. This finding underscores once again the generally negative correlates of part-time employment for fathers, perhaps for reasons noted earlier—cultural norms that see the male as breadwinner and the possibility that part-time schedules for men in this sample may represent an involuntary reduction in working hours. Interestingly, men who became fathers between 1968 and 1974 were more likely to report psychological exhaustion in 1974 if their wives were employed, whether full or part time. But this was no longer the case by 1981 for men who became fathers between 1974 and 1981, suggesting that the role strains of two-earner couples had indeed been reduced. Sandqvist (1987a) found in her study of U.S. and Swedish fathers that they had a higher involvement in child-care when their wives were employed. While this may lead to greater role overload for fathers it can also enhance their self-esteem and general well-being (see also Baruch and Barnett, 1986; Barnett and Baruch, 1987).

So few of the women who became mothers between the 1974 and 1981 surveys were out of the labor force in 1981 ($N = 35$) that it is difficult to paint a clear picture of the factors affecting their well-being. But being a single parent or living in a large city both indisputably contributed to less positive appraisals of life circumstances.

Parenthood and Well-Being: Conclusions

Becoming a parent is associated with higher levels of well-being for Swedish women in 1981 than was the case in 1968. But a number of family and occupational conditions enhance or exacerbate that well-being. Participation in the labor force, per se, does *not* contribute to psychological distress or fatigue for women making the transition to motherhood. Rather, the *conditions* of their employment matter most: part-time hours are conducive to lower levels of fatigue and distress and a more positive evaluation of life conditions. Family structure is also a determining factor, with single-parent mothers particularly vulnerable to psychological distress and fatigue.

Men who became fathers in 1981 had higher levels of fatigue and psychological distress than did those who became fathers in the latter part of the 1960s. Workplace conditions also affect the well-being of men making the transition to fatherhood, but in a distinctive manner. For first-time fathers, not working hours but the ability to leave the job for brief periods promotes well-being. And this could be reflective of a broader sense of autonomy on the job.

Low- and High-Risk New Mothers

Statistical analyses reported in Chapters 3 and 5 documented the significance of previous psychological distress or fatigue in rendering a parent at risk for continued symptoms and underscored the vastly different experiences of high- and low-stressed individuals (see, e.g., Figure 5.2). Here I seek the factors that might affect the existing level of well-being of women who became mothers between surveys. When high levels of distress are experienced before motherhood, what circumstances reduce such symptoms? Or, conversely, what are the conditions under which once stress-free individuals come to experience, concomitant with motherhood, fatigue or psychological distress?

This section systematically examines the impact of previous levels of well-being, looking at two cohorts of women (1968–74 and 1974–81) who made the transition to parenthood within two survey periods. The analysis concentrates on these women since (1) they have recently undergone a major life change (motherhood) with repercussions for every facet of their lives and (2) they are the group that must grapple most extensively with the cross-pressures of work and family roles.

Low-Risk Mothers: The 1968–74 Cohort

There were 121 women who in 1968 experienced neither symptoms of psychological distress nor feelings of fatigue and who became mothers between 1968 and 1974. About two-thirds (65 percent) of these "low-risk" new mothers were in the labor force and 27 percent had left the labor force by 1974. Their average age in 1974 was 28.6 years; by this time they had, on average, 1.5 children. Four percent lived with neither a husband nor a cohabitant, and 15 percent had a husband working more than 40 hours a week.

Which of these low-risk women were likely to experience either psychological distress or daily fatigue by 1981, following their movement into motherhood? Age is clearly an important factor in reducing the likelihood of both distress and fatigue (see Table 6.3). The low-risk women who delayed childbearing are *more* likely to continue experiencing high levels of well-being than are their younger counterparts. But moving either into or out of the labor force does not in itself contribute to changes in these women's well-being.

Turning now to the 72 low-risk mothers who were employed in 1974, we find that 15 percent were on leave of absence and half were working part time. Only 3 percent were putting in more than 40 hours a week.

These low-risk women were more likely to report feelings of fatigue by 1974 if they were in professional occupations. The typical pressure of these jobs, in conjunction with the added pressures of a family, are apparently key contributors. This finding is somewhat surprising, since generally it has been the women in professional and managerial occupations who have exhibited the highest levels of well-being. Marital status, again, affected psychological distress, single parents being more likely than those with husbands or partners to report symptoms of psychological strain by 1974.

Four factors that *reduced* the likelihood of fatigue were: age (becoming a mother later rather than earlier in life), a spouse working more than 40 hours a week, being on a leave of absence, and working part time. Why should a woman whose husband works overtime be less likely to experience fatigue? It may be that women whose husbands fulfill the traditional provider role by working longer hours experience reduced pressure to be family breadwinners as they become mothers. The fact that women who curtail their employment, whether through leaves or working part-time, are less likely to complain of fatigue lends support to this hypothesis.

Table 6.3. Factors affecting various measures of well-being for first-time mothers, employed and with low levels of previous reported strain

	1974 ($N = 72$)		1981 ($N = 96$)	
	Psychological distress	Daily fatigue	Psychological distress	Daily fatigue
Individual and family characteristics				
Age		–		–
Education				
Physical limitations				
Residence				
Metropolitan				
Rural				
Family size				+
Marital status				
Single parent	+		+	
Working hours and scheduling				
Part-time		–		
Overtime				+
Leave last week		–		
Spouse part-time				
Spouse overtime		–		
Working environment				
Physical pressures, t1				+
Physical pressures, t2				+
Psychological pressures, t1			+	+
Psychological pressures, t2				+
Occupational level				
Upper class		+		
Working class				
Self-direction				
Autonomy				
Sets own pace				
R^2	.06	.117	.124	.242

Source: 1974, 1981 waves of the Level of Living Survey, Swedish Institute for Social Research, Stockholm University.

Note: + (–) = Factors statistically significant in contributing to higher (lower) levels of psychological distress and daily fatigue. t1 = 1974; t2 = 1981.

Low-Risk Mothers: The 1974–81 Cohort

Of the 108 women who became mothers between 1974 and 1981 and who reported neither strains nor fatigue prior to childbearing, the great majority (89 percent) by 1981 were in the labor force and only 7 percent had left it. The average age of these women in 1981 was 30.8 years, slightly higher than that of the 1968–74 cohort. Fewer in this cohort (12 percent compared to 15 percent) had spouses working more than 40 hours a week and a slightly larger proportion (6 percent compared to 4 percent) lived with niether a spouse nor a cohabitant. As with the earlier low-risk cohort, employment per se made no difference in these women's well-being by the time of the second survey. Of those who were employed, two-thirds (62.5 percent) were working part time and almost a fourth (23 percent) were on leaves of absence.

As with the 1968–74 cohort, *marital status* as much as characteristics of the job is related to psychological distress among the 96 employed women in this cohort in 1981. Understandably, women without the support of a spouse or partner are more vulnerable to psychological strains. Jobs with high psychological pressures also contribute to distress.

Working hours are an important contributor to fatigue; as one would expect, those working more than 40 hours a week are most likely to report feelings of fatigue. Moreover, in this 1974–81 cohort the physical and psychological pressures of the job promote fatigue in working mothers. This was not true for the 1968–74 subgroup, and it underscores the increasing significance of conditions of work in affecting women's well-being. As with the 1968–74 cohort, age reduces the likelihood of fatigue. This suggests that women who somewhat delay their childbearing and who experience high levels of well-being prior to the birth of their child do not find the meshing of work and family roles quite so tiring as do younger women.

High-Risk Mothers: The 1968–74 Cohort

What about high-risk first-time mothers? In the 1968–74 cohort, 55 women who became parents by 1974 reported high levels of both fatigue and strain in 1968. Twenty-seven percent of these had left the labor force by 1974 and 49 percent were currently employed that year. Nine percent were single parents, compared with the 4 percent of low-risk mothers in this category.

These women made the transition to motherhood when they were already experiencing high levels of fatigue and psychological distress. Yet those who *left* the labor force between 1968 and 1974 were more likely to report fatigue than those who had remained out of the labor force from the beginning. These may have been women who found it too difficult to combine work and family roles, whether because of heavy family or workplace responsibilities. On the other hand, those who had been employed in 1968 and continued to work following childbearing were more likely to report psychological distress. Thus, among women with low levels of well-being in 1968 who became parents by 1974, neither continued employment nor leaving the labor force offered a ready solution to the stresses in their lives.

Unfortunately, there are too few high-risk mothers ($N = 18$) who were employed at the time of the 1974 survey to examine the conditions of employment that might have affected their well-being. However, note that in this group none were on leave and fewer than 40 percent were working part-time. Sixty percent experienced psychological pressures at work and half had jobs requiring a great deal of physical exertion. This contrasts with the job situation of the low-risk mothers in this cohort, only 36 percent of whom had physically or psychologically demanding jobs. Clearly the conditions of employment of these women do not seem conducive to well-being, given earlier findings about the importance of working hours and job pressures.

Note also that these women are typically younger (average age twenty-seven in 1974) than the women in the low-risk group (average age thirty in 1974). We already have seen that, for the low-risk groups in both the 1968–74 and 1974–81 cohorts, the younger mothers are likely to experience lower levels of well-being.

High-Risk Mothers: 1974–81 Cohort

Fifty-three women who became mothers between 1974 and 1981 had reported feelings of both psychological distress and fatigue in 1974. These high-risk new mothers were 28.5 years of age on average in 1981, and 11 percent were single parents. Three-fourths (75.5 percent) were in the labor force in 1981, and 11 percent had left the labor force between 1974 and 1981. In the sample of 40 employed high-risk mothers, fully a third were on leave at the time of the 1981 survey and almost two-thirds (65 percent) worked part-time.

Given relatively low levels of well-being prior to childbearing, what factors contribute to the well-being of these women following the transition to motherhood? As far as fatigue is concerned, little seems to matter—neither employment status nor, for those in the labor force, any configuration of occupational conditions reduces the likelihood of fatigue. In the case of psychological distress, women who report physical health limitations are most likely to continue reporting symptoms of psychological strain. For this subgroup, remaining in the labor force *reduces* the likelihood of symptoms of psychological distress among high-risk mothers; but a job that is mentally taxing *increases* the probability of continued distress. Being on a leave of absence, however, reduces these symptoms. Again, working conditions play an important role in promoting or detracting from the well-being of women who become mothers.

Optimal Conditions for Parenting

Few agree about conditions that are optimal for a high "quality of life" or "well-being," but there is general consensus about those conditions that *impair* it. Psychological distress and daily fatigue are certainly not conducive to optimal well-being or high-quality parenting. In this chapter I have aimed to explore forces that are *conducive* to well-being. In particular, this last section assesses the conditions under which women who experienced psychological strains and fatigue before motherhood show diminished symptoms afterwards, and looks at the factors that help to keep women with high levels of well-being at the same high levels following motherhood.

The data permits us to draw a portrait of "successful" mothers, those who manage the often competitive demands of work and family roles without reporting symptoms of psychological distress or daily fatigue. For women who have a history of well-being, the background factors that seem to matter most are marital status and age. Women who raise their children with the support of a spouse or partner (most commonly the father) are far more likely to continue experiencing well-being. Similarly, those who somewhat delay childbearing appear to manage the transition to motherhood, in conjunction with employment, better than do younger mothers.

But certain workplace conditions also promote or detract from the well-being of these less vulnerable women: working hours affect fatigue, and, by 1981, the physical and psychological pressures of work also produce fatigue.

For high-risk women, that is, those who reported both distress and fatigue prior to the birth of a child, there are significant cohort differences. Among women becoming mothers between 1968 and 1974, fatigue (in 1974) was greater for those leaving the labor force and symptoms of distress (in 1974) more common for those remaining in the labor force. But for the second cohort, those giving birth between 1974 and 1981, the likelihood of psychological distress was actually reduced for those remaining in the labor force. The specific condition of employment that led to a reduction in strains by 1981 was the leave of absence. This finding suggests that, especially for high-risk women entering motherhood, the parental benefits expanded through legislation in the 1970s played a vital role in improving maternal well-being during the childbearing years.

7

Conclusions and Implications

If we have little reason to conclude that equality is at hand, let us at least rejoice that we are marching in the right direction. (Goode, 1982, p. 1)

Interconnections between Work and Family

The ties between work and family constitute a fertile ground for analyzing the links between macro (societal) and micro (individual) events. Large-scale social changes in gender-role prescriptions, which are occurring in all advanced societies, and innovative social policies such as those adopted in Sweden invariably modify the interconnections between the institutions of the family and the workplace. But these links also represent contingencies in the lives of individual men and women trying to make a living and raise their families as best they can. This book addresses the significance of these historical transformations in the work–family nexus for parents of young children.

To what extent do alterations in the prevalence of maternal employment and new directions in labor market and family policies affect the well-being of those living in the midst of these changes? We know that the stress experienced in work inevitably spills over into family life by influencing the overall emotional health of the worker. We know too that family stress necessarily intrudes into the workplace to the degree that it also colors a worker's psychological well-being (Crouter, 1984; Piotrowski and Crits-Cristoph, 1982). But is the level of parental well-being improving or deteriorating, and what specific factors are related to it?

To understand the sources of stress and well-being one must examine

ioth as they exist at a particular moment and as they
e (Pearlin, 1980). Young adults, in their early years of
l child-rearing, have been found to experience more psy-
ss than during any other life stage, as they cope with
occupational pressures and uncertainties while simultaneously immers-
ing themselves in marital and family roles and responsibilities (Campbell, 1981; Pearlin, 1982, 1983; Fernandez, 1985; Gerson, 1985). But it is
not clear whether the strains experienced by these young parents have
been increasing or declining with the widespread changes in gender roles
occurring over the past several years.

Nowhere have the legal and social norms regarding gender equality
been more deliberately shaped than in Sweden. Nowhere is more
assistance given to working parents in the form of parental leaves,
reduced working hours, and other social supports. And nowhere in the
western world has a larger proportion of mothers of young children
entered and remained in the labor force. Hence, I have focused on working parents in Sweden as an exemplary case of the lifestyle embodied in
contemporary parenting.

My interest has been in the personal well-being of Swedish parents, in
analyzing stability and change in the emotional health of those who
cared for young children in the critical years from 1968–1981. These parents carried out their childcare responsibilities in vastly different milieus,
created by both the societal transformation of gender role prescriptions in
the 1970s toward greater equality and the social policies adopted to facilitate the meshing of work and family roles. The changes in women's roles
in Sweden in the 1970s—particularly through the labor force participation of mothers of preschoolers—may well foretell the experiences we in
the United States will face in the 1990s.

Several major themes emerge from the findings of this study.

Gender Differences

Regardless of the measure used, Swedish mothers consistently reported
lower levels of well-being than did fathers from 1968 to 1981. Specifically, mothers of young children were more likely than were fathers to
report fatigue and psychological distress in all three surveys. Thus,
women continue disproportionately to bear both the burden of childcare
and the strains seemingly endemic to the early years of adulthood.

There are, in addition, significant differences in the employment experiences of working mothers and fathers. Although the gender gap in earnings has been reduced substantially, working men and women in
Sweden, as elsewhere, continue to be concentrated in quite different
jobs. In fact, gender segregation in the occupational structure is greater

in Sweden than in the United States. One consequence of this occupational segregation, as well as unequal family responsibilities, is that women and men commonly work under different conditions of employment. Particularly striking are differences in hours spent at work. A majority of mothers of young children work less than full time whereas the great majority of fathers continue to put in a standard work week.

Although I was not able to study single-parent fathers—they were too few in number—I found that single-parent (noncohabiting) mothers in Sweden are particularly stressed. Marital status, even more than working conditions, is linked to well-being, with mothers lacking partners the most vulnerable to distress and fatigue. This finding is consistent with that of research in the United States which documents the strains experienced by divorced women (Downey and Moen, 1987; Menaghan and Lieberman, 1986; Weitzman, 1985). Especially interesting in the Swedish case is the fact that this vulnerability persists despite the considerable economic and social supports made available to single parents in that country.

But parental well-being overall depends on *both* work and family situations, with the specific factors affecting it differing by gender. Many working conditions, such as psychological pressures, influence the well-being of both men and women, but others affect one more than the other. For example, part-time schedules reduce the fatigue of mothers but not fathers. And the well-being of fathers is enhanced, in particular, by their autonomy on the job, in being able to easily leave work for brief periods. Furthermore, the likelihood that men will experience distress is also reduced by the fact that many of their wives are employed part time.

Differences over Time

I used two principal measures to gauge stability and change in well-being from 1968 to 1981: (1) a checklist of symptoms of psychological distress experienced over the past year, and (2) reported feelings of fatigue over the two preceding weeks. Swedish mothers were less likely to report psychological distress in 1981 than in 1974 and 1968, but there was no counterpart trend in distress among fathers. However, a significant change did occur over the thirteen-year period in fathers' feelings of fatigue. Controlling for background variables, I found that there was an increase in the likelihood of fathers reporting daily fatigue from 1968 to 1981. The proportion of mothers experiencing fatigue, on the other hand, remained relatively steady, even declining slightly by 1981, especially for women in the labor force.

These findings raise a number of questions regarding the changing roles of men and women during this period of Swedish history. In 1968 a minority (36 percent) of Swedish mothers with young children were in the labor force, while nearly 80 percent were employed by 1981. Yet, contrary to a role strain hypothesis, this substantial change appears not to have resulted in a significant decline in their level of well-being. In fact, it actually improved from the late 1960s to the early 1970s.

By 1981 participation in the labor force alone appears neither to exacerbate nor mitigate the psychological distress and fatigue experienced by Swedish women. There are several possible explanations for the improvement in maternal well-being that go beyond their increased labor force participation per se. One is that role overload for employed mothers in Sweden is precluded or reduced by the availability of both part-time employment and extended leaves of absence for the care of infants. Indeed, the Level of Living data indicate that relatively few mothers in Sweden were actually on the job in a full-time capacity. Most were in the labor force, to be sure, but on leaves of absence or working part time. Their improved well-being may well testify to the effectiveness of these and other social supports provided to working women in Sweden.

Another factor that may have eased the burden of employed mothers could have been a redistribution of childcare responsibilities between parents. Unfortunately, I was unable to document the time that each parent devoted to child care. Still, the fact that a larger proportion of Swedish fathers reported feelings of daily fatigue by 1981, even though their working hours had been considerably reduced after 1968, suggests at least the possibility that they assumed a somewhat larger share of the childcare responsibility. But since relatively few fathers took advantage of parental leave options and the vast majority of them worked full time, their involvement in childcare continued to be limited by their time spent in employment as well as by enduring norms regarding the mother as the principal caretaker of the children. However, the fact that fathers at all occupational levels were given increasing latitude on the job suggests a degree of flexibility that may have permitted them to assume a slightly larger share of the childcare responsibility.

Yet another explanation of the reduced strains of Swedish mothers could be that the psychological benefits of employment for women, in the form of an enhanced role identity, more than compensate for the overloads employment creates in their lives, thereby producing little net change in the proportion experiencing strains. Indeed, the fact that a majority of mothers are employed part time suggests that for many Swedish women the positive value of employment is maximized while its negative effects, especially its time constraints, are considerably reduced.

The finding of increased feelings of fatigue, from 1968 to 1981, among fathers of young children may seem surprising since their average work week was markedly reduced during this thirteen-year period. I tested whether this was causally related to the increase in women's labor force participation, using panel data. For men who reported fatigue in 1974, wives' employment did increase the likelihood of continued fatigue in 1981. However, for husbands who did not report fatigue in 1974 the employment of their wives actually reduced its probability in 1981. Thus, a wife's employment seems to exacerbate already existing fatigue, not to generate fatigue by itself. But the narrowing difference in fatigue between mothers and fathers of young children may reflect the larger trend toward equalization of men's and women's roles within Swedish society generally, rather than a specific response to a wife's employment.

Differences by Social Class and Workplace Conditions

Social class turns out to be even more important than historical time period as a predictor of psychological distress for parents. Working-class mothers were the most likely to report psychological distress, whether or not they were employed. In contrast, fathers in professional occupations were most apt to experience distress. These differences by socioeconomic level remained stable throughout the three time periods studied.

Parental well-being seems to be a product of a complex set of forces, including work role demands, position in the socioeconomic structure, and previous level of well-being. Although women's participation in the labor force per se may not have any measurable effects, specific aspects of employment can either exacerbate or mitigate the overloads they experience and influence the well-being of both parents.

There is, consequently, much more to employment than the mere fact of labor force participation, the variable most typically used in studies of mothers with young children. Employment for some parents involves the performance of physical tasks; for others the tasks are principally mental in nature. For a significant minority the physical and psychological demands of the job are substantial; for others they are modest or minimal.

These surveys did not contain data on a number of potentially influential job conditions, such as the social nature of the job—the opportunities it affords for interpersonal relations and cooperation among workers—and the interest value of the work itself. However, the measures that were available do lend confidence to the conclusion that the conditions of work differ by gender and class, and that they have differential effects on well-being. Monotonous jobs, for example, lead to psychological distress and are much more common in working-class occupations. Jobs described as "mentally taxing" also produce symptoms of distress, and men in professional and managerial positions are most apt to characterize their jobs as taxing. More generally, working-class jobs seem related to the experience of fatigue, particularly among working mothers, beyond the specific occupational characteristics included in this study. Thus, location in the occupational hierarchy gives rise to distinctive job experiences and has clear implications for personal well-being.

Life Stage Differences

In this study I focus specifically on the experiences and feelings of parents with young children present in the home, the life stage when parents must grapple with strong and simultaneous demands on their time and energy by both their work and their families. One of the conundrums that parents face is the fact that families, particularly those with young children present, are inherently both absorptive (requiring time, energy and commitment) and "nonbureacractic"—many care-giving tasks within the family are neither uniform nor predictable, and activities cannot be ordered and regulated as they would be in more formal organizations (Litwak and Figuera, 1969). These are tasks that can best be handled by parents and in some cases only by parents. As such, they cannot easily be set aside or put out of mind during working hours.

I found few life stage differences in well-being. In other words, the well-being of recent parents is not strikingly different from that of other parents who had preschoolers or those whose preschoolers had moved into the middle childhood years by the time of the second survey. One trend is evident, however: older fathers tend to report higher levels of psychological distress and, in the case of recent parents, older mothers exhibit less distress. Finally, controlling for marital status and previous strains, women who recently became first-time mothers were more vulnerable to distress than those who already had children.

This study highlights two principal ways by which working parents with young children seem best able to cope, at least in safeguarding their own well-being. The first is by reducing their time involvement in employment. Women working part time rather than full time were less apt to report feelings of fatigue or symptoms of psychological distress. This arrangement, along with parental leaves of absence, was especially important in reducing the strains experienced by high-risk new mothers, that is, women who gave birth to their first child in the period between the 1974 and 1981 surveys and who reported high levels of fatigue and strain in 1974. Husbands whose wives worked part time also benefitted, but those with less than full-time hours themselves were more prone to distress.

The second mode of adaptation consists of those mechanisms that permit parents to better discharge their family responsibilities during working hours by providing considerable latitude on the job. Freedom to leave the job for brief periods when necessary enables parents to meet their family's needs and unanticipated exigencies. This flexibility is critical to parenting. Jobs that afford parents more control in allocating their time between work and home are also more conducive to their well-being. This is not to say that decision latitude is less valuable for workers at other life stages. Indeed, research has convincingly established its importance for workers of all ages (Karasek, 1979, 1981; Levi, 1974; Levi et al., 1982; House et al., 1979). But these time options are particularly critical to working parents, who consistently report long and inconvenient hours as significant contributors to personal and family strain (Pleck, 1983, 1985; Staines and Pleck, 1983; Fernandez, 1985; Galinsky, 1987; Willer, 1986).[1]

Societal Differences

Sweden was the first nation to adopt, in 1968, a policy of sex-role equality, striving for a parallelism in the roles of men and women to replace the traditional sexual division of labor. It also was the first country to acknowledge the need to change men's work roles in order to bring about more than a semblance of gender equality (Scott, 1982). As such, it has been on the cutting edge of social change. However, the findings of this study suggest that Swedish men and women raising children continue to differ both in the nature of their employment experience, including its time requirements, and in their levels of well-being. Moreover, though I find the disparities in fatigue and psychological distress between men and women are narrowing, these differences seem unlikely to disappear in the near future.

How comparable are the experiences reported here to those of working parents in the United States? Unfortunately, no data archive analogous to the Level of Living Survey exists in the United States. But recent studies of the mental health of men and women generally do suggest certain similarities. First, women more than men in America, as in Sweden, continue to report higher levels of distress. Also like Sweden, this gender difference appears to be declining in the United States. And third, working less than full time seems to contribute to the well-being of working mothers in both countries.

What is markedly different between Sweden and the United States are

---

1. Another potential source of support for working parents is the provision of child care by the government. However, available day care services do not yet meet the escalating demand. Parents are frequently put on waiting lists for their children's day care, which itself may be a source of distress. However, the effects of day care on parental well-being could not be addressed with the data available in the Level of Living Survey.

available to working parents as they begin the years of child-
٫ and child-rearing. A majority of Swedish mothers use a "combination strategy" of part-time employment and paid parental leave to
maintain their tie to the labor force while devoting time to childcare
(Bernhardt, 1987a, b; Sundström, 1987). (Although Swedish fathers
have these same benefits, few utilize them.) In contrast, comparatively
few parents in the United States enjoy the opportunity or can afford to
take parental leave following the birth of a child or to reduce their normal
working hours to care for their preschool children. American parents
who cannot afford to purchase full-time childcare or domestic services
must deal with the work–family dilemma by having the mother either
leave the labor force for some, often protracted, period of time or shift to
a part-time job that is frequently less secure and offers lower wages and
fewer benefits than does full-time employment (Moen, 1985; 1986). Most
American families at this life stage juggle their work and family obligations ad hoc, as best they can. This juggling act frequently leads to a
sequence of work and family crises and prevents women, who are the
principal jugglers, from performing optimally in either role (Fernandez,
1985; Galinsky, 1987). However, in the United States, as in Sweden, having a wife tailor her work involvement to changing family needs does
permit husbands/fathers to concentrate their time and energy on their
jobs and to continue in their traditional breadwinner role.

Sweden and the United States also differ in public attitudes regarding
the proper roles of men and women. Trends toward egalitarianism are
common to both countries, but a significant proportion of Americans
continue to support the traditional division of labor between the sexes,
and many who do espouse the principle of gender equality are often quite
conventional in structuring their own lives (Komarovsky, 1976, 1985;
Rubin, 1980; Berk, 1985). The absence of a national consensus about
gender roles has been a major impediment to the adoption of institutional
supports for working parents in the United States.

Theoretical Implications

The life course perspective guiding this evaluation of the well-being of Swedish parents attends to the interface of two central trajectories across adulthood: the occupational career and the parenting "career." And these in turn
are tied to still a third trajectory: shifts in emotional well-being throughout
adulthood. The life course orientation focuses on how these progressions
have changed historically, how they differ among various subgroups
within society, and how they are shaped by life contexts and contingencies.

The Significance of Context

Historical change inevitably alters these contexts and contingencies. And, indeed, I found that social and demographic changes occurring during the 1970s in Sweden had significant implications for the well-being of parents. A confluence of forces—maternal employment, cultural norms upholding gender equality, legislation benefitting working parents—has resulted in narrowing the gap in the well-being of women and men raising young children. But the mechanisms by which these changes have taken place are complex. Women's propensity for psychological distress declined from 1968 to 1981, but not simply as a result of their greater labor force participation. Rather, the conditions of their employment—such as part-time hours and leaves of absence—mattered more than employment per se. And the likelihood of men experiencing fatigue increased from 1968 to 1981, but not simply as a result of their wives' employment. It is true that men already reporting fatigue in the 1974 survey were more likely to be fatigued in 1981 if their wives were employed. But those without fatigue in the 1974 survey who had employed wives were less likely to be fatigued in 1981. Attention to such considerations of context invariably introduces complexity. But, while a life course orientation does offer rich insights, it does not promise simple explanations.

Another aspect of context involves earlier experiences that shape the course of lives as well as patterns of psychological health. I found the dynamics of well-being to include a certain "cumulativeness": individuals experiencing psychological distress and fatigue in one survey are the most prone to these difficulties in the next survey. Life changes such as becoming a parent, moving into or out of the labor force, or having a wife work must be considered within this background of emotional resources; those who previously do well are less prone to problems.

Among the other contextual resources shown to temper well-being is age or, more specifically, the timing of motherhood. Women who delay childbearing seem to have a greater propensity for well-being than those having children earlier in adulthood. Still another resource is the emotional support of a partner, whether a spouse or a cohabitant. Single mothers, lacking this support, are particularly disadvantaged. And for men, the emotional gratification of children may reduce their susceptibility to distress; those with more children evidence less distress.

Social class groupings also constitute socially structured contexts for work, parenting and well-being. I found that the occupational hierarchy establishes the job conditions and gratifications that, in conjunction with family conditions, can promote or detract from well-being. But the most critical contextual factor affecting parental well-being is gender.

Gender as Context

Social systems use gender as a fundamental basis for social organization. Nowhere is this more significant than when individuals become parents. At no time in the life course are the divisions between men and women more marked. And, despite the changing sociocultural context regarding gender equality, cultural norms persist in defining parenting in terms of sex-appropriate behavior. Women are taking on new roles in the marketplace without abandoning old roles and old expectations in the home (see also Berk, 1985; Coverman and Sheley, 1986).

The findings of this study call for more thought, more discussion and certainly more research concerning these ongoing changes in men's and women's roles. The study does not support the all too common assumption that the increased labor force participation of mothers of young children leads perforce to an increase in stress. Certainly there is no support for the role-strain hypothesis, which suggests that by adding employment to their family roles women will experience psychological distress and fatigue as a result of their role overloads and conflicts. Despite widespread changes in the labor force participation of Swedish women during the 1970s, there has been no corresponding decrease in maternal well-being. To the contrary, the well-being of mothers of young children actually appears to have improved over this time.

But neither does this study affirm the multiple-roles hypothesis which holds that employment per se should improve women's well-being. Merely being in or out of the labor force does not account for changes in psychological distress or fatigue from one survey to the next. What matters are family conditions and conditions at work. Moreover, aside from the finding that Swedish fathers reported more fatigue in 1981 than in 1968, it is the mothers of young children who continue to bear a disproportionately large share of the childcare burden, and mothers, even in a socially progressive country like Sweden, who continue to experience higher levels of fatigue and psychological strain than do fathers.

The emerging life course paradigm for the psychological effects of women's employment argues for the simultaneous consideration of many elements. Any differences in well-being by employment status may be a composite function of four sets of factors: (1) self-selection—those individual predispositions and experiences drawing women into or out of the labor force; (2) conditions of work, including the time at work and workplace flexibility as well as the job's physical and psychological demands; (3) structural options, such as parental leaves and work-time reduction, as well as the larger opportunity structure within the labor market that pushes or pulls women into or out of the labor force and the cultural context which defines maternal employment positively or negatively; (4) family situation, including the number and ages of children as well as the presence of a spouse and, for women, the timing of motherhood. The findings of this study direct attention to the dynamic interplay among these elements in promoting or reducing well-being. The challenge to research is to develop more complete theoretical accounts of the contingent nature of women's well-being, how their altered roles and behavior patterns produce stress, and how stress, in turn, produces alterations in roles and behavior patterns. Such theoretical models would be complex, to be sure, but they would also offer a more comprehensive representation of reality.

On the subject of differences between men and women, the statistical analyses illustrate unmistakable shifts in the distribution of well-being by gender, concomitant with converging gender roles. These data are also consistent with the historical trends documented in studies of U.S populations, and suggest that the circumstances of parenting in both countries have changed considerably. These findings, too, suggest the need for more complex theoretical models. Current explanations of gender differences tend to ignore historical context as well as the life contexts of work and family conditions. Gender differences in well-being are narrowing among Swedish parents, but in part because fathers are increasingly reporting fatigue. And the declining psychological distress of mothers must be couched with reference to the structural supports legislated in the 1970s.

Any model seeking to explain gender differences must incorporate the social, economic, and political contexts in which they are embedded. Thus, the issue of the relationship between gender and well-being is broadened to include historical context as well as conditions at home and at work. Theoretical models must move beyond a limited role-strain or multiple-role orientation to focus on the trajectory of well-being over time, in a shifting sociocultural context. This more complicated but more enriched view should help to unravel the web of forces linking gender, family, employment, and well-being.

The Role of Public Policy: Lessons for the United States

To be truly rational, it is necessary to accept the obvious principle that a social program, like a practical judgment, is a conclusion based upon premises of value as well as upon facts. (Alva Myrdal, 1971, p. 1)

We in the United States live in an era of radical change in gender roles, a period marked by unprecedented ambiguity and uncertainty but also opportunity. The 1990s undoubtedly will see more, not fewer, mothers of young children in the labor force, increasing the complexity not only of family life but also of working life and, consequently, of our society as a whole. What is required to prepare for this imminent future are public policies that can lessen, for both men and women, the cross-pressures of work and family roles.

How transferable are the policies of Sweden to other nations? In particular, to what extent can the Swedish actions to achieve gender equality in parenting and in employment be regarded as policy prescriptions for the United States? To be sure, Sweden is a small, relatively homogeneous country of little more than eight million people, a number roughly equal to those residing in metropolitan New York. And among Swedes there is a commitment to collectivism and a general acceptance—although with some recent reservations—of the high taxes required to support their extensive social welfare system. Americans, on the other hand, historically have had a strong ideological commitment to the ethic of individualism and the tenets of the free enterprise system (see, e.g., Gilder, 1981), and they have been notably reluctant to pay the costs of significantly expanded government benefits and services. Obviously, then, the cultural and political context of parenting and employment is markedly different in the two nations.

Yet there also are some similarities between Sweden and the United States which cannot be denied. In both countries it is women who bear the primary burden of reconciling work and parenting roles. In both countries fathers devote many more hours to employment than do mothers. Although American women have not entered or remained in the labor force in the same proportions as have Swedish women, over half of all U.S. mothers of preschoolers are now employed, and the fastest growing group among them consists of mothers with infants under one year of age. Fathers and mothers in both countries are grappling with the ambiguities now surrounding gender roles. What it means to be a man or a woman within the family or on the job no longer has the same clarity that it did only a few decades ago.

Nevertheless, the United States continues to make labor market policy "as though 'worker' is a masculine noun" (Cook, 1978, p. 50). Employed mothers in the United States are expected to "make it" under present rules and conditions, coping as best they can. American fathers are expected to sustain their primary investment in work. But the practice of both parents taking on the traditional male work role—each working full-time and not taking time off to meet childcare needs—would be patently unacceptable in Sweden. Although most Swedes value work and occupational achievement as highly as most Americans, they value home and family to an even greater extent. From the Swedish viewpoint, women cannot merely be assimilated into the traditional male world of work. Rather, this world must be recast in ways that permit fathers as well as mothers to participate equitably in the "production" of human beings and mothers no less than fathers to participate equitably in the production of goods and services.

Ideology versus Reality

As we have seen in this study, equality, even in Sweden, remains as much an ideal as a reality, despite the major social and legislative efforts made over the years to achieve equality. The discrepancy between ideology and reality is due far less to employment options and occupational choices than to the still unequal responsibilities for home and family shouldered by men and women. And this in turn suggests that the achievement of equality requires not only legislated employment benefits for working parents, but something more—a marked redistribution of parenting responsibilities between men and women.

Oakley (1974, 1981) suggests that the adequate fulfillment of work and family obligations is impossible insofar as success in one often implies failure in the other. Sweden's social arrangements have attempted to facilitate the management of both roles, of making the impossible possible. This ideological commitment is deeply entrenched in Swedish society. In the course of my research I met no Swede—male or female, young or old, high- or low-status—who did not at least express the conviction that both parents should and could continue their employment during the early child-rearing years.

But, as we have seen, it is primarily Swedish women who continue to balance domestic and employment responsiblities. Although the numbers are gradually changing, it is mothers rather than fathers who most often take parental leaves in Sweden, and who take them for longer periods of time. And it is predominantly mothers rather than fathers who opt for reduced work schedules while their children are young. The likely price women pay, in terms of their own career and personal development, cannot be ignored (e.g., Barrett, 1979; Bielby and Baron, 1986; Coverman, 1983). The "combination strategy" that Swedish women have adopted (Bernhardt, 1987a,b), one foot in the home and one in the labor market, may seem compelling in the short run as a means of meeting family demands, but it necessarily reinforces gender differences, and it may well limit women's job and advancement options as employers anticipate that women are likely to be on leave or part time. This updated model of the traditional division of labor—in which women remain in the labor force following childbearing but in part-time and frequently secondary positions—in no way represents the achievement of gender equality.

But to say this is not to understate the very impressive accomplishments of Sweden in developing and supporting opportunities for individuals to function simultaneously as workers and as parents. Sweden remains the world's indisputable leader in imaginatively inventing and implementing gender-free structural supports for working parents.

Implications for the United States

Sweden's progressive policies offer an impressive lesson on how advanced societies can further the cause of equality between the sexes. But the Swedish model cannot be transferred *in toto* to another country. Unlike Sweden, the United States is neither small nor relatively homogeneous. By no means are all Americans comfortable with the changing roles of men and women. And certainly many are not pleased with the proliferation of women—especially mothers of young children—in the labor force. But at the same time there should be little doubt that our already substantial maternal employment is not going to wane. Although the Swedish "model" in its entirety cannot be adopted in the United States, what can be more deliberately propagated if not emulated are the values underlying Swedish policies, including an explicit goal of gender equality and a deep commitment to helping parents meet the needs of their children.

Many of the issues raised here regarding the experiences and well-being of working parents are vitally important and deserve close attention. By framing issues of employment policy with specific reference to the needs of working parents, the United States can begin to address today's (and tomorrow's) realities, rather than cling to a vision of the American family and American society that is rapidly becoming outdated. What Sweden provides then is not a grand blueprint to follow but a promising new perspective and some concrete examples of ways to deal with critical issues of work and family life whose resolution in the United States is a matter of growing urgency.

The Workplace and Families: The Nature of Postindustrial Society

Never before has the tension been so evident or the room for maneuver so narrow. After two hundred years of development, both the future of the family and the fulfillment of women as persons are at odds as never before. (Degler, 1980, p. 473)

The roles of men and women are undergoing a progressive transformation in all advanced societies, but the rate of change among them varies considerably. Understandably, the more highly developed countries have advanced the furthest in the sex role revolution (Davis, 1984). The trend toward gender equality endemic to modernity is simply more pronounced in Sweden than elsewhere. The issues raised by the transformation of gender roles are becoming more prominent and pressing as the full import—for the family, for the workplace, and, indeed, for the whole of society—of this push toward equality is coming to be understood and appreciated.

But in the search for ready solutions to complex problems there is invariably a danger of oversimplification. As Daniel Bell warns, "the most grievous mistake in the social sciences is to read the character of a society through a single overarching concept . . . and to mislead one as to the complex (overlapping and even contradictory) features of any modern society, or to assume that there are 'laws of social development' in which one social system succeeds another by some inexorable necessity" (1976, p. xii). The intricacies of modern life and the very real distinctions between Sweden and other countries are not to be discounted.

Clearly the multiple links among employment, parenting, and well-being are neither simple nor self-evident; however, these linkages constitute a critical issue in all advanced industrialized societies in contemporary times. What Sweden provides is a note of caution. Misunderstandings about the future of American families, and particularly narrow and misleading definitions of what does or should constitute a "typical" family, detract attention from the very real dilemmas of working parents in the United States.

The goal is not to reject the past in favor of the present, but to reaffirm the values of family and home within the changing context of modern society. A policy agenda that can support families in all their forms and at all their life stages is not easy to construct. But clearly it requires variable "life-cycle" solutions that address the particular needs of parents of young children in all types of family settings.

The findings reported here underscore the unevenness of social change across socioeconomic groupings, but especially by gender. The creation of parallel roles, with men and women carrying out both work and family responsibilities, is a formidable challenge. The traditional assignment of tasks, obligations, and rewards by gender is not easily transformed, even when official ideology and structural changes are directed to this goal. One cannot simply mandate gender equality—whether in terms of employment conditions, degree of work involvement, or personal feelings of well-being—so long as there is a decided inequality in the assump-

tion of childcare and household responsibilities. And prevailing inequalities in employment cannot help but reinforce the traditional sexual division of labor in domestic life. Kingsley Davis (1984) put it succinctly: "the
obvious remedy for this weakness [of the egalitarian system] is to equalize
the rights and obligations of the two sexes in both the workplace and the
home" (p. 413).

Sweden's experience illustrates that there are constraints and perhaps
even limits in achieving equality. But possibly the most instructive lesson
to be learned from the Swedish example is that various means can be
legislated to reduce, albeit not eradicate, the historical inequality
between men and women and to facilitate an optimal and equitable sharing of work and family responsibilities. The well-being of Swedish mothers was at a measurably higher level in 1981 than it was in 1968, even
though mothers were still more likely than fathers to evidence symptoms
of distress and fatigue. Clearly the gap between the two appears to be
closing. Moreover, in 1981 mothers were more likely to be employed,
fathers were more likely to be working fewer hours, and, as a consequence of new public policies, both were given opportunities to reduce
their work loads in the face of parental obligations. By no means do these
change constitute a fully egalitarian society, but they do represent significant progress in reducing the sharp distinctions by gender (Skard and
Haavio-Mannila, 1984).

Still another word of caution: it is important that we do not make the
mistake of equating equality with sameness and thereby using the male
role to gauge the status and progress of women (Giele, 1978, 1980; Holter,
1970; Rossi, 1984). Instead, what is required are alternative patterns of
working and parenting that are not specific to either gender, and
especially structural conditions of employment that can be adapted to
changing family needs over the life cycle.

Sweden's experience offers not so much a solution as an action-oriented
declaration of intent. That country's commitment to gender equality
continues to drive its policy development, as is evident in the ongoing
debate about the adoption of a six-hour working day for all employees as
an additional means of enabling parents to spend more time with their
children (LO, 1983, 1987). By contrast, we in the United States, individually and collectively, remain uncertain, if not divided, as to what
men's and women's roles should be—a degree of irresolution hardly conducive to formulating a coherent public policy.

Yet the momentum toward egalitarianism that seems to be an inevita-
ble byproduct of the demographic and social changes accompanying
postindustrialism can neither be ignored nor arrested. New norms
regarding the roles of men and women at work and at home will have to

be fashioned to conform more closely to this emerging reality. Sweden has taken an important step in this direction; it provides a useful point of reference for discussions in the United States of new policy options that can meet the needs of working parents. Through its deliberate reconstruction of norms for working and parenting, Sweden has established guidelines and structures that encourage men and women to follow more parallel roles with regard to workplace and family.

Appendices
References
Index

Appendix A

The *Daily Fatigue* Index is a Guttman-type scale ranging from 1 to 8, constructed from the following items:

The following four questions concern your health during the past *two weeks:*

U163   Have you often felt tired *during the past two weeks?*
U164   Do you have difficulty getting started in the morning?
U165   Have you felt particularly tired during the day?
U166   Have you felt extremely tired in the evening?

The *Psychological Distress* Index is a Guttman-type scale ranging from 1 to 5, constructed from the following items:

Have you during the past 12 months had any of the following ailments or illnesses? (items presented with a range of common physical complaints)

U216   General tiredness
U217   Sleeplessness
U218   Nervous trouble (anxiety, uneasiness, fear)
U219   Depression

The *Quality of Life* measure is based on the following item:

U702   We have asked you a whole lot of questions about the quality of your life. How would *you* evaluate your situation? On the whole, would you say that your life conditions are very good, quite good, rather bad, or very bad?

1 Very good
2 Quite good
3 Neither good nor bad
4 Rather bad
5 Very bad

The *Physical Exhaustion* measure is based on the following item:

U450   Do you often feel physically exhausted when you come home from work?

The *Psychological Exhaustion* measure is based on the following item:

U454   Do you often feel mentally exhausted when you get home from work?

Appendix B

Variables included in regression equations:

Individual Characteristics
    Age (in years)
    Education (1 = some university education)
    Physical Limitation (1 = trouble in taking a brisk 100-meter walk, in running 100 meters, in climbing and descending stairs.
    Social Class
        Upper (professionals, executives)
        Lower (steel workers and other manufacturing workers, construction workers, service workers, agricultural workers)
        (Omitted category) Middle (technical and clerical workers, foremen, farmers, small proprietors, government white-collar nonprofessional employees)
    Residence
        Metropolitan (Stockholm, Göteborg, Malmö)
        Rural (rural area or village of not more than 500 people)
        (Omitted category) Midsize (small and medium-sized towns)
    Previous Strain (score on Psychological Distress scale in preceding survey)
    Previous Fatigue (score on Fatigue scale in preceding survey)

Family Characteristics
    Number of Children (actual number reported)
    Family Stage
        New Parents (those with no children preceding survey)
        Middle Childhood (those with preschoolers preceding survey, with only school-aged children present survey)
        (Omitted category) Preschoolers Both Years (those having preschoolers both in preceding and present survey)
    Marital Status (1 = women with neither cohabitant nor husband)

Working Hours and Scheduling
    Part-Time Hours (1 = employed less than 35 hours a week)
    Overtime (1 = employed more than 40 hours a week)

Shiftwork (1 = nonregular schedule, either night, evening, early morning,
  two or more shifts, or irregular shifts
Leave Last Week (1 = on leave of absence week preceding survey)
Leave Last Year (1 = on leave of absence during year preceding survey)
Spouse FT (1 = spouse employed 35–40 hours a week)
Spouse PT (1 = spouse employed less than 35 hours a week)
Spouse OT (1 = spouse employed more than 40 hours a week)
(Omitted category) OLF (spouse not in labor force)—father sample
Spouse FT—mother sample

Job Demands
Physical Pressures t1 (1 = required to lift 60 kilos or job in other ways physically demanding, preceding survey)
Physical Pressures t2 (1 = required to lift 60 kilos or job in other ways physically demanding, current survey)
Psychological Pressures t1 (1 = job mentally taxing, hectic or monotonous,
  preceding survey)
Psychological Pressures t2 (1 = job mentally taxing, hectic or monotonous,
  current survey)

Occupational Level
Upper (1 = same as social class, above)
Lower (1 = same as social class, above)
Spouse Upper (1 = husband in upper-level occupation)
Spouse Lower (1 = husband in lower-level occupation)

Self-Direction
Autonomy (1 = If you need to go on a private errand, can you leave your
  workplace for about half an hour without informing your
  supervisor?)
Sets Own Pace (1 = Can you yourself decide your pace of work?)
Punctuality (1 = Is punctuality demanded at your workplace?)

Other Control Variables
Wage Rate (hourly wage)
Job Experience (years spent in employment)

References

Åberg, R. 1987. Working conditions. In Erikson, R., and Åberg, R. (Eds.), *Welfare in transition: A survey of living conditions in Sweden 1968-1981* (pp. 102-116). Oxford: Clarendon Press.

Åberg, R., Selén, J., and Thom, H. 1987. Economic resources. In Erikson, R., and Åberg, R. (Eds.), *Welfare in transition: A survey of living conditions in Sweden 1968-1981* (pp. 117-153). Oxford: Clarendon Press.

AIC. *See* International Centre of the Swedish Labour Movement.

Aldous, J., and Hill, R. 1969. Breaking the poverty cycle: Strategic points for intervention. *Social Work*, 14:3-12.

Aldous, J., Osmond, M., and Hicks, M. 1979. Men's work and men's families. In Burr, W., Hill, R., Reiss, I., and Nye, F. I. (Eds.), *Contemporary theories about the family* (pp. 227-256). New York: Free Press.

Allardt, E. 1976. Work and political behavior. *Handbook of work, organization and society*. Chicago: Rand McNally.

Anderson, G. 1986. The Swedish man. *Inside Sweden*, No. 3-4 (June):13.

Andersson, S. O. 1981. *The Swedish labour movement*. Stockholm: International Centre of the Swedish Labour Movement (AIC).

Aneshensel, C. S., Frerichs, R. R., Clark, V. A. 1981. Family roles and sex differences in depression. *Journal of Health and Social Behavior*, 22:379-393.

Ariès, P. 1962. *Centuries of childhood: A social history of family life*. Translated by Robert Baldick. New York: Knopf.

Axel, H. 1985. *Corporations and families: Changing practices and perspectives*. Research Report No. 608. New York: The Conference Board.

Barnett, R., and Baruch, G. K. 1985. Women's involvement in multiple roles and psychological distress. *Journal of Personality and Social Psychology*, 49:135-145.

Barnett, R., and Baruch, G. K. 1987. Determinants of fathers' participation in family work. *Journal of Marriage and the Family*, 49(1):29-40.

Barrett, N. S. 1979. Women in the job market: Occupations, earnings, and career opportunities. In Smith, R. E. (Ed.), *The subtle revolution* (pp. 31-61). Washington, DC: The Urban Institute.

Baruch, G. K., and Barnett, R. C. 1986. Fathers' participation in family work: Parents' role, strain, well-being. *Journal of Personality and Social Psychology*, 51:981-991.

Baude, A. 1983. *Public policy and changing family patterns in Sweden 1930-1977*. Working Paper No. 6. Stockholm: Arbetslivscentrum.

Belsky, J., Lerner, R. M., and Spanier, G. B. 1984. *The child in the family.* Reading, MA: Addison-Wesley.

Berk, S. F. 1985. *The gender factory: The apportionment of work in American households.* New York: Plenum Press.

Bernard, J. 1972. *The future of marriage.* New York: World.

Bernard, J. 1981. The good provider role: Its rise and fall. *American Psychologist,* 36(1):1–12.

Bernhardt, E. M. 1987a. *The choice of part-time work among Swedish one-child mothers.* Stockholm Research Reports in Demography, No. 40. Stockholm: University of Stockholm.

Bernhardt, E. M. 1987b. *Labour force participation and childbearing: The impact of the first child on the economic activity of Swedish women.* Stockholm Research Reports in Demography, No. 41. Stockholm: University of Stockholm.

Bielby, W., and Baron, J. 1986. Women and work: Sex segregation and statistical discrimination. *American Journal of Sociology,* 91:759–799.

Boethius, M. 1984. *The working family.* Social Change in Sweden, No. 30. Stockholm: Swedish Information Service.

Bohen, H. H. 1983. *Corporate employment policies affecting families and children: The United States and Europe.* New York: The Aspen Institute.

Bohen, H. H., and Viveros-Long, A. 1981. *Balancing jobs and family life: Do flexible work schedules help?* Philadelphia: Temple University Press.

Brim, O. G., Jr., and Kagen, J. (Eds.). 1980. *Constancy and change in human development.* Cambridge, MA: Harvard University Press.

Bronfenbrenner, U. 1979. *The ecology of human development.* Cambridge, MA: Harvard University Press.

Bronfenbrenner, U. 1982. The context of development and the development of context. In Lerner, R. M. (Ed.), *Developmental psychology: Historical and philosophical perspectives* (pp. 147–230). Hillsdale, NJ: Erlbaum Associates.

Bronfenbrenner, U. 1986. Ecology of the family as a context for human development: Research perspectives. *Developmental Psychology,* 22:723–742.

Bronfenbrenner, U., and Crouter, A. C. 1982. Work and family through time and space. In Kamerman, S. B., and Hayes, C. D. (Eds.), *Families that work: Children in a changing world* (pp. 39–83). Washington, DC: National Academy Press.

Brown, G. W., and Harris, T. 1978. *Social origins of depression: A study of psychiatric disorders in women.* New York: Free Press.

Bureau of National Affairs. 1986. *Work and family: A changing dynamic.* Washington, DC: Bureau of National Affairs.

Burke, R. J., and Weir, T. 1976. Relationship of wives' employment status to husband, wife and pair satisfaction and performance. *Journal of Marriage and the Family,* 38:278–287.

Burnley, J. 1985. All women are equal but some are more equal than others. *Sweden Now,* 19(3):24–26.

Campbell, A. 1981. Changes in psychological well-being during the 1970's of homemakers and employed wives. In McGulgan, D. G. (Ed.), *Women's lives:*

New theory, research and policy (pp. 291–301). Ann Arbor, MI: University of Michigan Center for Continuing Education of Women.

Campbell, A., Converse, P. E., and Rodgers, W. J. 1976. *The quality of American life.* New York: Russell Sage.

Catalyst. 1986. *Report on a national study of parental leaves.* New York: Catalyst.

Cherlin, A. 1981. *Marriage, divorce, and remarriage.* Cambridge, MA: Harvard University Press.

Cleary, P., and Mechanic, D. 1983. Sex differences in psychological distress among married people. *Journal of Health and Social Behavior,* 24:111–121.

Coleman, J. S. 1986. Social theory, social research and a theory of action. *American Journal of Sociology,* 91(6):1309–1335.

Coleman, R. P., and Rainwater, L. 1978. *Social standing in America: New dimensions of class.* New York: Basic Books.

Colletta, N. 1979. Support systems after divorce: Incidence and impact. *Journal of Marriage and the Family,* 41:837–845.

Cook, A. 1978. *Working women: European experience and American need.* Ithaca, NY: School of Industrial and Labor Relations. Cornell University. Reprint Series, No. 431.

Coser, R., and Rockoff, G. 1971. Women in the occupational world: Social disruption and conflict. *Social Problems,* 18:535–554.

Cott, N. E., and Pleck, E. H. 1979. *A heritage of her own: Toward a new social history of American woman.* New York: Simon and Schuster.

Coverman, S. 1983. Gender, domestic labor time and wage inequality. *American Sociological Review,* 48:123–137.

Coverman, S., and Sheley, J. F. 1986. Change in men's housework and child care time 1965–1975. *Journal of Marriage and the Family,* 48 (May):259–272.

Crouter, A. C. 1984. Spillover from family to work: The neglected side of the work family interface. *Human Relations,* 37(6):425–442.

Crouter, A. C., and Perry-Jenkins, M. 1986. Working it out: Effects of parental work on parents and children. In Vogman, M. W., and Brazelton, T. B. (Eds.), *Stresses and supports for families* (pp. 93–108). Cambridge, MA: Harvard University Press.

Dahlström, E., and Liljeström, R. 1969. The family and married women at work. In Dahlström, E. (Ed.), *The changing roles of men and women.* Translated by G. Anderman and S. Anderman. Boston: Beacon Press.

Daniels, P., and Weingarten, K. 1982. *Sooner or later: The timing of parenthood in adult lives.* New York: W.W. Norton & Co.

Davis, K. 1984. Wives and work; The sex role revolution and its consequences. *Population and Development Review,* 10(3):397–417.

Davis, K., and van den Oever, P. 1982. Demographic foundations of new sex roles. *Population and Development Review,* 8(3):495–511.

Degler, C. N. 1980. *At odds: Women and the family in America from the Revolution to the present.* New York: Oxford University Press.

Dempster-McClain, D., and Moen, P. 1989. Moonlighting husbands: A life-cycle perspective. *Work and Occupations.*

Dohrenwend, B. P., and Dohrenwend, B. S. 1969. *Social status and psychological disorder.* New York: John Wiley.

Dohrenwend, B. P., and Dohrenwend, B. S. 1976. Sex differences and psychiatric disorders. *American Journal of Sociology,* 81:1447–54.

Dohrenwend, B. P., and Dohrenwend, B. S. 1977. The conceptualization and measurement of stressful life events: An overview of the issues. In Strauss, J. S., Baibigian, H. M., and Roff, M. (Eds.), *The origins and course of psychopathology* (pp. 135–186). New York: Plenum Press.

Dohrenwend, B. P., Shrout, P. E., Egrl, G., and Meidelsohn, F. S. 1981. Nonspecific psychological distress and other dimensions of psycholopathology. *Archives of General Psychiatry,* 37:1229–1236.

Downey, G., and Moen, P. 1987. Personal efficiency, income, and family transitions: A longitudinal study of women heading households. *Journal of Health and Social Behavior,* 28:320–333.

Ekdahl, B. 1984. *Child custody rules in the context of Swedish family law.* Social Change in Sweden, No. 31 (November). Stockholm: Swedish Information Service.

Elder, G. H., Jr. 1974. *Children of the Great Depression.* Chicago: University of Chicago Press.

Elder, G. H., Jr. 1975. Age differentiation and the life course. *Annual Review of Sociology,* 1:165–190.

Elder, G. H., Jr. 1978. Family and the life course. In Haraven, T. (Ed.), *Transitions: The family and the life course in historical perspective* (pp. 17–64). New York: Academic Press.

Elder, G. H., Jr. 1984. Families, kin and the life course: A sociological perspective. In Parker, R. D. (Ed.), *Review of child development research 7. The family* (pp. 80–136). Chicago: University of Chicago Press.

Elder, G. H., Jr. 1985. *Life course dynamics: Trajectories and transitions, 1968–1980.* Ithaca, NY: Cornell University Press.

Elder, G. H., Jr., and Rockwell, R. C. 1979. The life-course and human development: An ecological perspective. *International Journal of Behavioral Development,* 2:1–21.

Enquist, P. O. 1984. The art of flying backward with dignity. *Daedalus,* 113(1):61–74.

Entwisle, D., and Doering, S. G. 1981. *The first birth: A family turning point.* Baltimore: Johns Hopkins University Press.

Erikson, R. 1987. The class structure and its trends. In Erikson R., and Åberg, R. (Eds.), *Welfare in transition: A survey of living conditions in Sweden 1968–1981* (pp. 19–42). Oxford: Clarendon Press.

Erikson, R., and Åberg, R. (Eds.). 1987. *Welfare in transition: A survey of living conditions in Sweden 1968–1981.* Oxford: Clarendon Press.

Erikson, R., Hansen, E. J., Ringen, S., and Uusitalo, H. (Eds.). 1987. *The Scandinavian model: Welfare state and welfare research.* Armonk, NY: M.E. Sharpe.

Espenshade, T. J. 1985. Marriage trends in America: Estimates, implications, and underlying causes. *Population and Development Review,* 11 (2):193–245.

Etzler, C. 1987. *Education, cohabitation and the first child: Some empirical findings from Sweden.* Stockholm Research Reports in Demography, No. 34. Stockholm: University of Stockholm.

Farel, A. N. 1980. Effects of preferred maternal roles, maternal employment and sociodemographic status on school adjustment and competence. *Child Development,* 51:1179–1186.

Favor, C. A. 1984. *Women in transition: Career, family and life satisfaction in three cohorts.* New York: Praeger.

Faxén, K-O. 1982. Wages, prices, and taxes in the 1980s. In Rydén, B., and Bergström, V. (Eds.), *Sweden: Choices for economic and social policy in the 1980s* (pp. 181–197). London: George Allen and Unwin.

Featherman, D. L. 1983. Life-span perspectives in social science research. In Baltes, P. B., and Brim, O. G., Jr. (Eds.), *Life span development and behavior* (Vol. 5, pp. 1–57). New York: Academic Press.

Feldberg, R., and Glenn, E. 1979. Male and female: Job versus gender models in the sociology of work. *Social Problems,* 26(5):524–538.

Fernandez, J. P. 1985. *Child care and corporate productivity.* Lexington, MA: Lexington Books.

Ferree, M. M. 1976. Working-class jobs: Housework and paid work as sources of satisfaction. *Social Problems,* 23:431–441.

Freeman, R. B., and Medoff, J. L. 1984. *What do unions do?* New York: Basic Books.

Friedman, D. E. 1986. *Families and work: Managing related issues.* New York: The Conference Board.

Fritzell, J. 1985. *Barnfamiljernas levnadsnivå.* Stockholm: Institute for Social Research, Stockholm University.

Galinsky, E. 1987. Corporate policies and family life. In Yogman, M., and Brazelton, T. B. (Eds.), *Stresses and supports for families.* Cambridge, MA: Harvard University Press.

Gardell, B. 1976. Reactions at work and their influence on nonwork activities. *Human Relations,* 29:885–904.

Gardell, B., and Aronsson, G. 1982. *The working environment for local public transport personnel.* Stockholm: Swedish Work Environment Fund.

Gardell, B., Aronsson, G., and Barklöf, K. 1982. *The working environment for local public transport personnel.* Stockholm: Swedish Work Environment Fund.

Gardell, B., and Johansson, G. 1981. *Working life: A social science contribution to work reform.* New York: John Wiley.

Gavron, H. 1966. *The captive wives: Conflicts of housebound mothers.* London: Routledge and Kegan Paul.

Gerson, K. 1985. *Hard choices: How women decide about work, career, and motherhood.* Berkeley: University of California Press.

Giele, J. Z. 1978. *Women and the future: Changing sex roles.* New York: The Free Press.

Giele, J. Z. 1980. Adulthood as transcendence of age and sex. In Smelser, N. S., and Erikson, E. H. (Eds.), *Themes of work and love in adulthood* (pp. 151–173). Cambridge, MA: Harvard University Press.

Gilder, G. 1981. *Wealth and poverty.* New York: Basic Books.

Ginsburg, H. 1983. *Full employment and public policy: The United States and Sweden.* Lexington, MA: Lexington Books.

Gladstone, L. W., Williams, J., and Belous, R. S. 1985. *Maternity and parental leave policies: A comparative analysis.* Congressional Research Service Report No. 85–148 G Gov, July 16, 1985.

Gold, D., and Andres, D. 1978a. Comparisons of adolescent children with employed and unemployed mothers. *Merrill-Palmer Quarterly,* 24:243–254.

Gold, D., and Andres, D. 1978b. Developmental comparisons between ten-year-old children with employed and nonemployed mothers. *Child Development,* 49:75–84.

Goode, W. I. 1960. A theory of role strain. *American Sociological Review,* 25:483–496.

Goode, W. I. 1982. Why men resist. In Thorne, B., with Yalom, M. (Eds.), *Rethinking the family* (pp.131–150). New York: Longman.

Gore, S., and Mangione, T. 1983. Social roles, sex roles, and psychological distress: Additive and interactive models of sex differences. *Journal of Health and Social Behavior,* 24:300–312.

Gove, W. R. 1972. The relationship between sex roles, marital status, and mental illness. *Social Forces,* 56:67–76.

Gove, W. R. 1984. Gender differences in mental and physical illness: The effects of fixed roles and nurturant roles. *Social Science and Medicine,* 19:77–91.

Gove, W. R., and Geerken, M. R. 1977. The effect of children and employment on the mental health of married men and women. *Social Forces,* 56:66–76.

Gove, W. R., Grimm, J. W., Motz, S. C., and Thompson, J. D. 1973. The family life cycle: Internal dynamics and social consequences. *Sociology and Social Research,* 57:182–195.

Gove, W. R., and Peterson, C. 1980. An update of the literature on personal and marital adjustment: The effect of children and the employment of wives. *Marriage and Family Review,* 3:63–96.

Gove, W. R., and Tudor, J. F. 1973. Adult sex roles and mental illness. *American Journal of Sociology,* 78:812–835.

Grønseth, E. 1972. The breadwinner trap. In Howe, L. K. (Ed.), *The future of the family* (pp. 175–191). New York: Simon and Schuster.

Gustafsson, S. 1984. Equal opportunity policies in Sweden. In Schmid, G., and Weitzel, R. (Eds.), *Sex discrimination and equal opportunity: The labour market and employment policy* (pp. 132–154). Aldershot, England: Gower.

Gustafsson, S., and Jacobsson, R. 1985. Trends in female labor force participation. *Journal of Labor Economics,* 3:S256–274.

Guttentag, M., Salasin, S., and Belle, D. 1980. *The mental health of women.* New York: Academic Press.

Haas, L. 1981. Domestic role sharing in Sweden. *Journal of Marriage and the Family,* 43 (November):957–969.

Haas, L. 1982. Parental sharing of child care tasks in Sweden. *Journal of Family Issues,* 3(3):389–412.

Haas, L. 1984. Determinants of role-sharing behavior: A study of egalitarian couples. *Sex Roles,* 7:747–760.

Haas, L. 1987. *Fathers' participation in parental leave*. Social Change in Sweden, No. 37 (November). Swedish Information Service.

Haavio-Mannila, E., and Kari, K. 1980. Changes in the life patterns of families in the Nordic countries. *Yearbook of Population Research* (Helsinki), 18:6–34.

Hadenius, S. 1985. *Swedish politics during the 20th century*. Stockholm: The Swedish Institute.

Hall, D.T. 1972. A model of coping with role conflict: The role behavior of college educated women. *Administrative Science Quarterly*, 17:471–489.

Hammarström, R., Näsman, E., and Nordström, K. 1983. Projekplan—Arbetslivet och barnen. Stockholm: Arbetslivscentrum.

Hareven, T. K. (Ed.). 1978. *Transitions: The family and the life course in historical perspective*. New York: Academic Press.

Hayes, C. D., and Kamerman, S. B. (Eds.). 1983. *Children of working parents: Experiences and outcomes*. Washington, DC: National Academy Press.

Hayghe, H. 1986. Rise in mothers' labor force activity includes those with infants. *Monthly Labor Review*, 109 (February):43–45.

Hill, C. R., and Stafford, F. P. 1980. Parental care of children: Time diary estimates of quality, predictability and variety. *Journal of Human Resources*, 15(2):219–239.

Hoem, B., and Hoem, J. M. 1987. *The Swedish family: Aspects of contemporary developments*. Research Reports in Demography, No. 43. Stockholm: University of Stockholm.

Hoffman, L. B. 1984. Work, family and the socialization of the child. In Parker, R. D. (Ed.), *Review of child development research 7. The family* (pp. 223–282). Chicago: University of Chicago Press.

Holland, J. 1980. *Women's occupational choice: The impact of sexual divisions in society*. Stockholm: Stockholm Institute of Education.

Hollingshead, A. A., and Redlich, F. C. 1958. *Social class and mental illness*. New York: John Wiley.

Holmes, T. H., and Rahe, R. H. 1967. The social readjustment rating scale. *Journal of Psychosomatic Research*, 11:213–218.

Holmstrom, L. L. 1973. *The two-career family*. Cambridge, MA: Schenkman.

Holter, H. 1970. *Sex roles and social structure*. Oslo, Norway: Universitets Forlaget.

House, J. S., McMichael, A. J., Wells, J. A., Kaplan, B. H., and Landerman, L. R. 1979. Occupational stress and health among factory workers. *Journal of Health and Social Behavior*, 20:139–160.

International Centre of the Swedish Labour Movement (AIC). 1981. *Swedish labour movement*. Stockholm: AIC.

Johansson, S. 1972. Conceptualizing and measuring welfare—Some experiences from the Swedish Low Income Committee. *Statistik Tidsdrift*, 2.

Johansson, S. 1973. The Level of Living Survey; A presentation. *Acta Sociologica*, 3:211–224.

Jonsson, J. 1987. Educational resources. In Erikson, R., and Åberg, R. (Eds.), *Welfare in transition: A survey of living conditions in Sweden 1968–1981* (pp. 154–180). Oxford: Clarendon Press.

Juster, F. T. 1985a. Investments of time by men and women. In Juster, F. T., and Stafford, F. P. (Eds.), *Time, goods, and well-being* (pp. 177–204). Ann Arbor, MI: University of Michigan Institute for Social Research.

Juster, F. T. 1985b. A note on recent changes in time use. In Juster, F. T., and Stafford, F. P. (Eds.), *Time, goods, and well-being* (pp. 313–332). Ann Arbor, MI: University of Michigan Institute for Social Research.

Kahn, R. 1981. *Work and health.* New York: John Wiley.

Kamerman, S. B. 1980. *Parenting in an unresponsive society: Managing work and family life.* New York: The Free Press.

Kamerman, S. B., and Hayes, C. D. 1982. *Families that work: Children in a changing world.* Washington, DC: National Academy Press.

Kamerman, S. B., and Kahn, A. J. 1981. *Child care, family benefits and working parents: A study in comparative policy.* New York: Columbia University.

Kamerman, S. B., and Kahn, A. J. 1987. *The responsive workplace: Employers and a changing labor force.* New York: Columbia University Press.

Kamerman, S. B., Kahn, A. J., and Kingston, P. 1983. *Maternity policies and working women.* New York: Columbia University Press.

Kandel, D., Davies, M., and Raveis, V. 1985. The stressfulness of daily social roles for women: Marital, occupational, and household roles. *Journal of Health and Social Behavior,* 26:64–78.

Kanter, R. M. 1977. *Work and family in the United States: A critical review and agenda for research and policy.* New York: Russell Sage.

Kaplan, H. B. 1983. *Psychosocial stress: Trends in theory and research.* New York: Academic Press.

Karasek, R. A., Jr. 1979. Job demands, job decision latitude, and mental strain: Implications for job design. *Administrative Science Quarterly,* 24:285–308.

Karasek, R. A., Jr. 1981. Job socialization and job strain: The implications of two related psychosocial mechanisms for job design. In Gardell, B., and Johansson, G. (Eds.), *Working life: A social science contribution to work reform* (pp. 75–94). New York: John Wiley.

Katz, D. A., and Kahn, R. L. 1978. *The social psychology of organizations* (2nd ed.). New York: John Wiley.

Keith, P. M., and Schafer, R. B. 1983. Employment characteristics of both spouses and depression in two-job families. *Journal of Marriage and the Family,* 45:877–884.

Kessler, R. C. 1979. Stress, social status and psychological distress. *Journal of Health and Social Behavior,* 20:259–272.

Kessler, R. C., and Cleary, P. D. 1980. Social class and psychological distress. *American Sociological Review,* 45:463–478.

Kessler, R. C., and McRae, J. A., Jr. 1981. Trends in the relationship between sex and psychological distress: 1957–1976. *American Sociological Review,* 46:443–452.

Kessler, R. C., and McRae, J. A., Jr. 1982. The effects of wives' employment on the mental health of married men and women. *American Sociological Review,* 47:216–227.

Kessler, R. C., and McRae, J. A., Jr. 1984. A note on the relationship of sex and marital status to psychological distress. In Greenley, J. A. (Ed.), *Research in community and mental health* (pp. 109–130). Greenwich, CT: JAI Press.

Kindlund, S. 1984. Family policy in Sweden. Paper presented at seminar, The Working Family: Perspectives and Prospects in the U.S. and Sweden, Washington, DC, May 1984, sponsored by Swedish Embassy.

Kingston, P. W., and Nock, S. L. 1985. Consequences of the family work day. *Journal of Marriage and the Family,* 47:617–629.

Kjellström, S. A., and Lundberg, O. 1987. Health and health care utilization. In Erikson, R., and Åberg, R. (Eds.), *Welfare in transition: A survey of living conditions in Sweden 1968–1981* (pp. 59–101). Oxford: Clarendon Press.

Kohn, M. L. 1977. *Class and conformity: A study of values* (2nd ed.). Chicago: University of Chicago Press.

Kohn, M. L. 1980. Job complexity and adult personality. In Smelser, N. J., and Erikson, E. H. (Eds.), *Themes of love and work in adulthood* (pp. 193–210). Cambridge, MA: Harvard University Press.

Kohn, M. L. 1987. Social stratification and transmission of values in the family: A cross-national assessment. *Sociological Forum,* 1(1):73–102.

Kohn, M. L., and Schooler, C. 1983. *Work and personality: An inquiry into the impact of social stratification.* Norwood, NJ: Ablex.

Komarovsky, M. 1976. *Dilemmas of masculinity: A study of college youth.* New York: W.W. Norton.

Komarovsky, M. 1985. *Women in college: Shaping new feminine identities.* New York: Basic Books.

Kornhauser, A. 1965. *Mental health of the industrial worker.* New York: Wiley.

Korpi, W. 1974. Poverty, social assistance and social policy in post-war Sweden. *Acta Sociologica,* 2–3:120–140.

Korpi, W. 1982. The historical compromise and its dissolution. In Rydén, B., and Bergström, V. (Eds.), *Sweden: Choices for economic and social policy in the 1980s* (pp. 124–141). London: Allen and Unwin.

Lamb, M. E. 1978. Influence of the child on marital quality and family interaction during the prenatal, perinatal, and infancy periods. Lerner, R. M., and Spanier, G. B. (Eds.), *Child influences on marital and family interaction: A life-span perspective.* New York: Academic Press.

Lapping, M. B. 1987. *University/industry cooperation to promote economic development in Sweden.* Working Life in Sweden, No. 33 (September). Stockholm: Swedish Information Service.

LaRossa, R., and LaRossa, M. M. 1981. *Transition to parenthood: How infants change families.* Beverly Hills, CA: Sage.

Lasch, C. 1977. *Haven in a heartless world: The family besieged.* New York: Basic Books.

Laslett, P., and Wall, R. (Eds.). 1972. *Household and family in past time.* Cambridge: Cambridge University Press.

Leighton, L., and Gustafsson, S. 1984. Differential patterns of unemployment in Sweden. *Research in Labor Economics,* 6:251–285.

Lein, L., Durham, M., Pratt, M., Schudson, M., Thomas, R., and Weiss, H.

1974. *Final report: Work and family life.* (NIE No. 3-3094). Wellesley, MA: Wellesley College Center for Research on Women.

Leiniö, T-L. 1988. Sex and ethnic segregation in the 1980 Swedish labor market. *Economic and Industrial Democracy*, 9(1): forthcoming.

LeMasters, E. 1957. Parenthood as crisis. *Marriage and Family Living*, 9:352-355.

Levi, L. 1974. Psychosocial stress and disease: A conceptual model. In Gunderson, E. K., and Rahe, R. H. (Eds.), *Life stress and illness* (pp. 8-33). Springfield, IL: Thomas.

Levi, L. 1978. *Quality of the working environment: Protection and promotion of occupational mental health.* Working Life in Sweden, No. 8. Stockholm: Swedish Information Service.

Levi, L., Frankenhauser, M., and Gardell, B. 1982. Report on work stress related to social structures and processes. In Elliott, G. R., and Eisdorfer, C. (Eds.), *Stress and human health* (pp. 119-146). New York: Springer.

Liem, R., and Liem, J. 1978. Social class and mental illness reconsidered: The role of economic stress and social support. *Journal of Health and Social Behavior*, 19:139-156.

Liljeström, R., and Dahlström, E. 1981. *Arbetarkvinnor i him- arbetssamhallsliv* (Working class women in home, work, and political life). Stockholm: Tiden.

Liljeström, R., Svensson, G. L., and Mellström, G. F., 1978. *Roles in transition.* Stockholm: Liber Forlag.

Litwak, E., and Figueira, J. 1968. Technological innovations and theoretical functions of primary groups and bureaucratic structures. *American Journal of Sociology*, 3:468-481.

LO. See Swedish Trade Union Federation.

Lundberg, O. 1986. Class and health: Comparing Britain and Sweden. *Social Science Medicine* 23:511-517.

MacLeod, D. 1984. *Why Sweden has better working conditions than the U.S.* Working Life in Sweden, No. 28 (April). Stockholm: Swedish Information Service.

Macmillan, A. M. 1957. The health opinion survey: Technique for estimating prevalence of psychoneurotic and related types of disorder in communities. *Psychological Reports*, 3:325-339.

Marini, M. M. 1980. Sex differences in the process of occupational attainment: A closer look. *Social Science Research*, 9:307-361.

Marks, S. R. 1977. Some notes on human energy, time and commitment. *American Sociological Review*, 42(6):921-936.

Mason, K. O., Czajka, J. L., and Arber, S. 1976. Change in U.S. women's sex-role attitudes, 1964-74. *American Sociological Review*, 41:573-596.

McLanahan, S., and Glass, J. 1985. A note on the trend in sex differences in psychological distress. *Journal of Health and Social Behavior*, 26:328-336.

Meissner, M. 1971. The long arm of the job: A study of work and leisure. *Industrial Relations*, 10:238-260.

Menaghan, E. G. 1983. Individual coping efforts: Moderators of the relationship between life stress and mental health outcomes. In Kaplan, H. B. (Ed.), *Psychosocial stress: Trends in theory and research* (pp. 157–194). New York: Academic Press.

Menaghan, E. G., and Lieberman, M. A. 1986. Changes in depression following divorce: A panel study. *Journal of Marriage and The Family*, 48:319–328.

Miller, J., and Garrison, H. H. 1982. Sex roles: The division of labor at home and in the workplace. *Annual Review of Sociology*, 8:237–262.

Miller, J., Schooler, C., Kohn, M. L., and Miller, K. A. 1979. Women and work: The psychological effects of occupational conditions. *American Journal of Sociology*, 85(1):66–94.

Ministry of Labor. 1985. *Side by side: A report on equality between women and men in Sweden 1985*. Stockholm: Gotab.

Ministry of Labor. Working Party for the Role of the Male. 1986. *The changing role of the male*. Stockholm: Ministry of Labor.

Mirowsky, J., and Ross, C. E. 1986. Social patterns of distress. *Annual Review of Sociology*, :23–45.

Modell, J., Furstenberg, F. F., Jr., and Hershberg, T. 1976. Social change and transitions to adulthood in historical perspective. *Journal of Family History*, 1:7–32.

Moen, P. 1982. The two-provider family. In Lamb, M. E. (Ed.), *Nontraditional families: Parenting and child development* (pp. 13–44). Hillsdale, NJ: Lawrence Eribaum Associates.

Moen, P. 1983. Unemployment, families and social policy: Forecast for the 1980's. *Journal of Marriage and the Family*, 45:751–760.

Moen, P. 1985. Continuities and discontinuities in women's labor force participation. In Elder, G. H., Jr. (Ed.), *Life course dynamics: 1960s to 1980s* (pp. 113–155). Ithaca, NY: Cornell University Press.

Moen, P. 1986. New patterns of work. In *Work and family: A changing dyk* (pp. 217–220). Washington, DC: Bureau of National Affairs.

Moen, P., and Dempster-McClain, D. 1987. Employed parents: Role strain, work time and preferences for working less. *Journal of Marriage and the Family*, 49(3):579an–590.

Moen, P., and Forest, K. 1989. The unevenness of social change: Employed parents in Sweden. Unpublished paper.

Moen, P., Kain, E. L., and Elder, G. H., Jr. 1983. Economic conditions and family life: Contemporary and historical perspectives. In *The high costs of living: Economic and demographic conditions of American families*. Washington, DC: National Academy of the Sciences.

Moen, P., and Moorehouse, M. 1983. Overtime over the life cycle: A test of the life cycle squeeze hypothesis. In Pleck, J. H., and Lopata, H. Z. (Eds.), *Research in the interweave of social roles: Jobs and families* (pp. 201–218). Greenwich, CT: JAI Press.

Moen, P., and Smith, K. R. 1986. Women at work: Commitment and behavior over the life course. *Sociological Forum*, 1(3):524–538

Moore, K. A., and Hofferth, S. A. 1979. Women and their children. In Smith, R. E. (Ed.), *The subtle revolution*. Washington, DC: The Urban Institute.

Mortimer, J. T. 1976. Social class, work and the family: Some implications for familial relationships and sons' career decisions. *Journal of Marriage and the Family*, 38 (May):241–256.

Mortimer, J. T., and Lorence, J. 1979. Work experience and occupational value socialization: A longitudinal study. *American Journal of Sociology*, 84(6):1361–1385.

Mortimer, J. T., Lorence, J., and Kuma, D. 1986. *Work, family, and personality: Transition to adulthood.* Norwood, NJ: Ablex.

Mott, P. E. 1965. *Shift work: The social psychology and physical consequences.* Ann Arbor, MI: University of Michigan Press.

Myrdal, A. 1941. *Nation and family: The Swedish experiment in democratic family and population policy.* London: Routledge and Kegan Paul.

Myrdal, A., and Klein, V. 1956. *Women's two roles: Home and work.* London: Routledge and Kegan Pauixuasman, E. 1986. Work and family: A combination made possible by part-time work and parental leave? Stockholm: Arbetslivscentrum. Unpublished.

National Central Bureau of Statistics (Statistiska Centralbyran). 1982. *Perspektiv pa valfarden* (Perspectives on Swedish welfare). Stockholm: National Central Bureau of Statistics.

National Committee on Equality between Men and Women. 1979. *Step by step: National plan of action for equality.* Stockholm.

Nock, S. L., and Kingston, P. W. 1984. The family work day. *Journal of Marriage and the Family*, 46:333–343.

Nock, S. L., and Kingston, P. W. Forthcoming. Time with children: The impact of couples' work-time commitments. *Social Forces*.

Oakley, A. 1974. *The sociology of housework.* London: Martin Robertson.

Oakley, A. 1981. *Subject: Women.* New York: Pantheon Books.

Oppenheimer, V. K. 1982. *Work and the family: A study in social demography.* New York: Academic Press.

Palme, O. 1970. The emancipation of man. Speech given at Women's National Democratic Club, Washington, DC.

Parsons, T. 1959. The social structure of the family. In Anshen, R. (Ed.), *The family: Its function and destiny.* New York: Harper.

Parsons, T., and Bales, R. 1966. *Family, socialization, and interaction process.* New York: Free Press.

Pearlin, L. I. 1975. Sex roles and depression. In Ginsberg, D. N. (Ed.), *Normative life crises* (pp. 191–207). New York: Academic Press.

Pearlin, L. I. 1980. The life cycle and life strains. In Blalock, H. M. (Ed.), *Sociological theory and research: A critical appraisal* (pp. 349–360). New York: Free Press.

Pearlin, L. I. 1982. The social contexts of stress. In Goldberg, L., and Breznitz, S. (Eds.), *Handbook of stress: Theoretical and clinical aspects* (pp. 367–379). New York: Free Press.

Pearlin, L. I. 1983. Role strains and personal stress. In Kaplan, H. B. (Ed.), *Psychosocial stress: Trends in theory and research* (pp. 3–32). New York: Academic Press.

Pearlin, L. I., and Johnson, J. S. 1977. Marital status, life-strains and depression. *American Sociological Review*, 42:104–115.

Pearlin, L. I., and Lieberman, M. A. 1977. Social sources of emotional distress. In Greenley, J. A. (Ed.), *Research in community and mental health*. Greenwich, CT: JAI Press.

Pearlin, L. I., Lieberman, M. A., Menaghan, E. G., and Mullan, J. T. 1981. The stress process. *Journal of Health and Social Behavior*, 22 (December):337–356.

Petersson, M., Dahlin, E., Gough, R., and Rhodin, L. 1982. *Deltids arbetet i Sverige*. Stockholm: Arbetslivscentrum.

Piotrkowski, C. S. 1979. *Work and the family system: A naturalistic study of working class and lower-middle class families*. New York: Free Press.

Piotrkowski, C. S., and Crits-Christoph, P. 1981. Women's jobs and family adjustment. *Journal of Family Issues*, 2(2):126–147.

Pleck, J. H. 1977. The work-family role system. *Social Problems*, 24:417–427.

Pleck, J. H. 1983. Husbands' paid work and family roles: Current research issues. In Lopata, H. Z., and Pleck, J. H. (Eds.), *Research in the interweave of social roles: Jobs and families* (pp. 251–333). Greenwich, CT: JAI Press.

Pleck, J. H. 1985. *Working wives, working husbands*. Beverly Hills, CA: Sage.

Pleck, J. H., and Staines, G. L. 1985. Work schedules and family life in two-earner couples. *Journal of Family Issues*, 6(1):61–82.

Pleck, J. H., Staines, G. L., and Lang, D. 1980. Conflicts between work and family life. *Monthly Labor Review*, 103(3):29–32.

Popenoe, D. 1986. *What is happening to the family in Sweden?* Social Change in Sweden, No. 366 (December). Stockholm: Swedish Information Service.

Popenoe, D. 1987. Beyond the nuclear family: A statistical portrait of the changing family in Sweden. *Journal of Marriage and the Family*, 49:173–183.

Presser, H. B., and Cain, G. G. 1983. Shift work among dual-earning couples with children. *Science*, 219:876–879.

Quinn, R. P., and Staines, G. L. 1979. *The 1977 Quality of Employment Survey: Descriptive statistics with comparison data from the 1969–70 and 1972–73 Surveys*. Ann Arbor, MI: University of Michigan Institute for Social Research, Survey Research Center.

Radloff, L. 1975. Sex differences in depression: The effects of occupation and marital status. *Sex Roles*, 1:249–265.

Radloff, L. 1977. The CES-D Scale: A self report depression scale for research in the general population. *Applied Psychological Measurement*, 1:385–401.

Rainwater, L. 1974a. *What money buys: Inequality and the social meaning of income*. New York: Basic Books.

Rainwater, L. 1974b. Work, well-being and family life. In O'Toole, J. (Ed.), *Work and the quality of life*. Cambridge, MA: MIT Press.

Rapoport, R., and Rapoport, R. N. 1975. The dual career family: A variant pattern and social change. *Human Relations*, 22:3–3.

Rich, S. 1987. Women's wages up sharply, easing gap. *Washington Post*, September 3:A1.

Robinson, J. P. 1985. Changes in time use: An historical overview. In Juster, F. T., and Stafford, F. P. (Eds.), *Time, goods and well-being* (pp. 289–312). Ann Arbor, MI: University of Michigan Institute for Social Research.

Ross, C. E., Mirowsky, J., II, and Huber, J. 1983. Dividing work, sharing work, and in-between: Marriage patterns and depression. *American Sociological Review*, 48 (December):809–823.

Ross, C. E., Mirowsky, J., II, and Ulbrich, P. 1983. Distress and the traditional female role: A comparison of Mexicans and Anglos. *American Journal of Sociology*, 89(3):670–682.

Rossi, A. S. 1968. Transitions to parenthood. *Journal of Marriage and the Family*, 30:26–38.

Rossi, A. S. 1984. Gender and parenthood. *American Sociological Review*, 49:1–19.

Rubin, L. 1980. *Worlds of pain: Life in the working-class family.* New York: Basic Books.

Ruggie, M. 1984. *The state and the working woman: A comparative study of Britain and Sweden.* Princeton, NJ: Princeton University Press.

Russell, S. 1974. Transition to parenthood: Problems and gratifications. *Journal of Marriage and the Family*, 36:294–302.

Rydén, B., and Bergström, V. 1982. Sweden in the 1980s: How gloomy are the prospects? In Rydén, B., and Bergström, V. (Eds.), *Sweden: Choices for economic and social policy in the 1980s* (pp. 1–8). London: George Allen and Unwin.

Sandqvist, K. 1987a. *Fathers and family work in two cultures.* Stockholm: Almqvist and Wiksell.

Sandqvist, K. 1987b. Swedish family policy and attempts to change paternal roles. In Lewis, C., and O'Brian, M. (Eds.), *Reassessing fatherhood: New observations on fathers and the modern family* (pp. 144–160). London: Sage Publications.

Scott, H. 1982. *Sweden's 'right to be human'. Sex-role equality: The goal and the reality.* Armonk, NY: M.E. Sharp.

Sieber, S. D. 1974. Toward a theory of role accumulation. *American Sociological Review*, 39:567–578.

Selén, J. 1985. Multidimensional descriptions of social indicators. *Social Indicators Research*, 16:541–581.

Shehan, C. 1984. Wives' work and psychological well-being: An extension of Gove's social role theory of depression. *Sex Roles*, 11(9/10):881–899.

Skard, T., and Haavio-Mannila, E. 1984. Equality between the sexes—myth or reality in Norden? *Daedalus*, 113 (1):141–168.

Smith, R. 1979. *The subtle revolution: Women at work.* Washington, DC: The Urban Institute.

Sokoloff, N. J. 1980. *Between money and love: The dialectic of women's home and market work.* New York: Praeger.

Staines, G. L. 1977. Work and nonwork: Part 1, A review of the literature. In Quinn, R. P. (Ed.), *Effectiveness in work roles*, Vol. 1. Ann Arbor, MI: University of Michigan, Institute for Social Research, Survey Research Center.

Staines, G. L., and Pleck, J. H. 1983. *The impact of work schedules on families.*

Ann Arbor, MI: University of Michigan Institute for Social Research, Survey Research Center.

Statistics Sweden. 1982. *Statistical abstract of Sweden 1982/83 (Statistisk arsbok 1982/83)*. Stockholm: Statistics Sweden.

Statistics Sweden. 1985. *Women and men in Sweden: Facts and figures*. Stockholm: Statistics Sweden (SCB).

Statuto, C. M. 1984. *Families in the eighties: Implications for employers (Part I)*. Department of Defense Family Studies. Washington, DC: Department of Defense, June.

Sundström, M. 1987. *A study in the growth of part-time work in Sweden*. Stockholm: Arbetslivscentrum.

Swedish Institute. 1983. *Swedish labor market policy*. Fact Sheets on Sweden. Stockholm: Swedish Institute, June.

Swedish Institute. 1984. *Equality between men and women in Sweden*. Fact Sheets on Sweden. Stockholm: Swedish Institute, May.

Swedish Institute. 1986. *Social welfare legislation in Sweden*. Fact Sheets on Sweden. Stockholm: Swedish Institute, January.

Swedish Institute. 1987a. *Higher education in Sweden*. Fact Sheets on Sweden. Stockholm: Swedish Institute, June.

Swedish Institute. 1987b. *Primary and secondary education in Sweden*. Fact Sheets on Sweden. Stockholm: Swedish Institute, June.

Swedish Trade Union Confederation (LO). 1983. *Working hours and employment*. Stockholm: Swedish Trade Union Confederation.

Swedish Trade Union Confederation (LO). 1987. LO and family policy. (Mimeo translated by Erica Stampa.) Stockholm: Swedish Trade Union Confederation, June.

Thoits, P. A. 1983. Multiple identities and psychological well-being: A reformulation and test of the social isolation hypothesis. *American Sociological Review*, 48:174–187.

Thoits, P. A. 1986. Multiple identities: Examining gender and marital status differences in distress. *American Sociological Review*, 51:259–272.

Thoits, P. A., and Hannan, M. 1979. Income and psychological distress: The impact of an income maintenance experiment. *Journal of Health and Social Behavior*, 20:120–138.

Thornton, A., and Freedman, D. 1979. Changes in the sex role attitudes of women, 1962–1977: Evidence from a panel study. *American Sociological Review*, 44(5):831–842.

Thornton, A., Alwin, D. F., and Camburn, D. 1983. Causes and consequences of sex-role attitudes and attitude change. *American Sociological Review*, 48:211–227.

Thurow, L. 1984. 62 cents to the dollar; the earnings gap doesn't go away. *Working Mother*, October:42.

Tröst, J. 1985. Marriage and nonmarital co-habitation. In Rogers, J., and Norman, H. (Eds.), *The Nordic family: Perspectives on family research*. Uppsala: Uppsala University, Department of History.

174

U.S. Bureau of the Census. 1984. *Marital status and living arrangements.* March 1983. Washington, DC: U.S. Government Printing Office.
U.S. Bureau of Labor Statistics. 1985. *News.* USDL 85-381. September 19, 1985.
U.S. Bureau of Labor Statistics. 1987. Over half of mothers with children one year old or under in labor force in March 1987. *News.* USDL 87-345.
Uhlenberg, Peter. 1980. Death and the family. *Journal of Family History,* 5:313-320.
Van Zandt Winn, S. 1984. Social class and income returns to education in Sweden: A research note. *Social Forces,* 62:1026-1034.
Verbrugge, L. M. 1983. Multiple roles and physical health of women and men. *Journal of Health and Social Behavior,* 24:16-30.
Veroff, J., Douvan, E., and Kulka, R. A. 1981. *The inner American: A self portrait from 1957 to 1976.* New York: Basic Books.
Vuksanović, M. 1975. *Kodbok för 1974 Års Levnadsnivå Undersökning.* Stockholm: Swedish Institute for Social Research.
Warr, P. B., and Parry, G. 1982. Paid employment and women's psychological well-being. *Psychological Bulletin,* 91(3):498-516.
Weitzman, L. 1985. *The divorce revolution.* New York: Free Press.
Welch, and Booth, A. 1974. Employment andian health among married women with children. *Sex Roles,* 3:385-397.
Wethington, E. 1987. Employment, family, and psychological distress: A study of married couples. University of Michigan, Ph.D. dissertation.
Wheaton, B. 1983. Stress, personal coping resources and psychiatric symptoms: An investigation of interactive models. *Journal of Health and Social Behavior,* 24:208-229.
Wilensky, H. L. 1960. Work careers and social integration. *International Social Science Journal,* 12:543-560.
Wilensky, H. L. 1981. Family life cycle, work, and the quality of life: Reflections on the roots of happiness, despair, and indifference in modern society. In Gardell, B., and Johansson, G. (Eds.), *Working life: A social science contribution to work reform* (pp. 235-263). New York: John Wiley.
Willer, B. 1986. An investigation of the work-family interface for families with young children. Cornell University, Ph.D. dissertation.
Wistrand, B. 1981. *Swedish women on the move.* Stockholm: Swedish Institute.
Women's Bureau, U.S. Department of Labor. 1983. *Time of change: 1983 handbook on women workers.* Bulletin 298. Washington, DC: U.S. Government Printing Office.
Women's Bureau, U.S. Department of Labor. 1985. *The United Nations Decade for Women 1976-1985.* Washington, DC: U.S. Government Printing Office.
Woods, M. B. 1972. The unsupervised child of the working woman. *Developmental Psychology,* 6(1):14-25.
Wright, J. D. 1978. Are working wives really more satisfied? Evidence from several national surveys. *Journal of Marriage and the Family,* 40:301-313.
Yarrow, M. R., Scott, P., De Leeuw, L., and Heinig, C. 1962. Childrearing in families of working and nonworking mothers. *Sociometry,* 25:122-140.
Young, M., and Willmott, P. 1973. *The symmetrical family.* New York: Pantheon.

Zaretsky, E. 1982. The place of the family in the origins of the welfare state. In Thorne, B. (Ed.), *Rethinking the family: Some feminist questions* (pp. 188–224). New York: Longman.

Zaretsky, E. 1976. *Capitalism, the family, and personal life.* New York: Harper and Row.

Zetterberg, H. L. 1984. The rational humanitarians. *Daedalus*, 113(1):75–92.

Index